ROUTLEDGE LIBRARY EDITIONS:
CHINA UNDER MAO

I0130401

Volume 11

RE-EDUCATING CHINESE
ANTI-COMMUNISTS

RE-EDUCATING CHINESE ANTI-COMMUNISTS

J.A. FYFIELD

Routledge
Taylor & Francis Group

LONDON AND NEW YORK

First published in 1982 by Croom Helm Ltd

This edition first published in 2019
by Routledge
2 Park Square, Milton Park, Abingdon, Oxon OX14 4RN

and by Routledge
711 Third Avenue, New York, NY 10017

Routledge is an imprint of the Taylor & Francis Group, an informa business

British Library Cataloguing in Publication Data
A catalogue record for this book is available from the British Library

ISBN: 978-1-138-32344-5 (Set)
ISBN: 978-0-429-43659-8 (Set) (ebk)
ISBN: 978-1-138-34108-1 (Volume 11) (hbk)
ISBN: 978-1-138-34109-8 (Volume 11) (pbk)
ISBN: 978-0-429-44036-6 (Volume 11) (ebk)

Publisher's Note
The publisher has gone to great lengths to ensure the quality of this reprint but points out that some imperfections in the original copies may be apparent.

Disclaimer
The publisher has made every effort to trace copyright holders and would welcome correspondence from those they have been unable to trace.

RE-EDUCATING CHINESE ANTI-COMMUNISTS

J.A. FYFIELD

CROOM HELM LONDON

ST. MARTIN'S PRESS NEW YORK

© 1982 J.A. Fyfield
Croom Helm Ltd, 2-10 St John's Road, London SW11

British Library Cataloguing in Publication Data
Fyfield, J.A.
    Re-educating Chinese anti-communists.
    1. Political socialization — China
    I. Title
    365'.66   HV9817
ISBN 0-7099-1017-7

All rights reserved. For information write:
St. Martin's Press, Inc., 175 Fifth Avenue, New York, N.Y. 10010
First published in the United States of America in 1982

Library of Congress Card Catalog Number 81-84061

ISBN 0-312-66733-7

Jacket illustration shows a political
re-education class in 1975. Courtesy
of the Anglo-Chinese Educational
Institute Ltd.

Printed and bound in Great Britain by
Biddles Ltd, Guildford and King's Lynn

CONTENTS

FOREWORD

To describe China is difficult, to interpret her a hazardous undertaking. The vocabulary that we are accustomed to use within our familiar conventions and in relation to countries like ours serves us poorly in writing about events, practices and policies in the People's Republic.

> To apply the same terms to a world that is unique in every respect — in its mentality, its traditional structures, its standard of living, and its chief problems — is to create a source of perpetual confusion. Ordinary words like 'liberty', 'family', and 'state' evoke entirely different ideas, attitudes, and duties in a Western and a Chinese. In the same way, the basic national purposes are totally dissimilar. If the Western goal is to raise our standard of living, for the Chinese, it is one of survival; this can change everything, even political morality.
>
> (Guillermaz, 1976: xx)

Guillermaz wrote this in 1972. Although China's declared national purpose is by now more comparable with that of advanced Western nations, his caution remains valid, especially as the events forming the substance of this book predate the modernization campaign launched in the late 1970s.

My first purpose in writing what follows has been to record the experiences, as told at first hand, of several men who, in the years before 1949, occupied military or government positions of influence, but for whom history must witness that, for all their influence, they failed in the struggle for power against the revolutionaries. For that failure, they spent long years in prison, finally, in most cases, to accept and to be accepted into a new role in the new society presided over by their former captors.

It has not been easy to set this account down without appearing to be an advocate for the system that permitted it, but my hope is that it has been accomplished with sufficient fairness for readers to make their own judgements uninfluenced by my own, if that is what they wish. Where I have gone further and attempted not only to present the point of view of the Communist leadership but also to explain and analyze it, this has been not with any intention to take sides but to assist in crossing the cultural boundary that might separate us from true understanding.

J.A. Fyfield

ACKNOWLEDGEMENTS

Encouragement from my colleagues of the Melbourne China Studies Group, notably Ronald Price, persuaded me to attempt this record.

Elaine Scott prepared the typescript with patience and care.

Claude Sironi assisted with the graphics.

The original project providing the material for the book was jointly planned and carried out with J.P. Hu and Myra Roper. The inspiration for it was Jerome Hu's alone and without that inspiration and his continued assistance this book could not have been written. He acted as interpreter at the interviews, gave advice on early drafts of chapters, helped in the translation of newspaper articles and supplied the Chinese characters for the glossary.

For the help of these people and the willingness of the publishers I am very grateful, although I do not wish to imply that the shortcomings are other than mine alone.

To reform an emperor into a self-supporting worker,
to reform war criminals into new people,
to change special agents and bandits from destroyers to constructors,
to reform professional burglars into new people who are willing to
   return money they have found, and
to transform the negative factors left over from the old society into
   positive factors for building socialism
are important achievements of great significance

(From an address by Xie Juezai, President of the Supreme People's
Court, to the National People's Congress in April 1960 (NCNA,
9 April 1960; trans. in *CB*, 624, 30 June 1960: 18-22))

Cure the sickness, to save the patient.

(Mao Zedong)

1 PRELIMINARIES

On 7 January 1979 J.P. Hu, Myra Roper and I arrived in Peking chasing an opportunity to investigate the re-education methods imposed by the Chinese Communist regime on high-ranking military and administrative personnel from the pre-1949 era. An opportunity to pursue this interesting question arose when J.P. re-established contact with his father, a former Guomindang official, after 26 years of silence. His father, imprisoned soon after Liberation for his alleged counter-revolutionary activities, had participated in a programme of re-education and had finally been released at the 1975 amnesty.

Hu Yunhong,[1] son of a village tailor in Jiangxi province, showed promise as a scholar and began his adult life as a schoolteacher. When one column of the National Revolutionary Army marching north from Canton on its northern expedition to eliminate the warlords and unify China arrived at Ruijin in the summer of 1926, Hu joined the army as a clerk. The army reached the Jiangxi capital, Nanchang, in November of that year. The commander of his division was a successful officer and distinguished politician who was subsequently appointed Governor of Jiangxi province. In this context of a successful army unit under a noted leader, it was possible for one like Hu, talented though lacking background, to rise to an important position.

It is significant for the understanding of Hu's future to ponder the situation into which he was moving: a situation marked by a degree of tension between Nationalist and Communist probably as severe as anywhere in China. Not only did the 1927 decision of the Nationalist Party to purge itself of the Communists probably have its origin in discussions at Nanchang (Kwei, 1970), but Nanchang was also the scene of the famous, if ill-fated, 1 August uprising led by Zhu De, marking the beginning of the open split between Communist and Nationalist and celebrated henceforward by the Communists as the birthday of the Red Army.

In this portentous milieu, Hu's position continued to rise and by the early thirties he was the chief secretary at division level in the Jiangxi Guomindang administration and head of its department of propaganda. It is thus he would have found himself in direct opposition to the Communists who now had the headquarters of their first soviet at Ruijin, ironically Hu's native town. On his arrest at the hands of the

1

Communists some 20 years later and during his subsequent long imprisonment, many of the allegations of bribery and corruption made against him related to this period in the thirties.

Hu must have feared that his life would be in danger if ever the Communists were to gain the upper hand; for, when in April 1949 the People's Liberation Army moved south of the River Yangtze (it reached Nanchang in May), he hastened with his second wife and family to Kunming in Yunnan province. Yunnan was still at that time under the control of the military governor, Lu Han, who gave allegiance to the Nationalist cause. When, however, Lu renounced this allegiance in December in favour of supporting the new government in Peking, Hu was stranded. He abandoned his family and went to neighbouring Sichuan province hoping that an acquaintance there might exercise some influence on his behalf in Peking, or that he might be able to rejoin the Guomindang. This move failed however. Chengdu was liberated by the People's Liberation Army. Hu was arrested in 1952, repatriated to his native Jiangxi for six months, and then imprisoned at Wuhan. In 1956 he was transferred to the Fushun prison in Liaoning province remaining there until released in March 1975.

It was only when the amnesty list was published in 1975 (NCNA, 24 March 1975) that J.P. discovered that his father had remained alive under the People's Republic. As a young man, J.P. himself had left Jiangxi in 1949, joining the exodus to Taiwan and eventually migrating to Australia, losing contact with his father and other members of his family. Now, following the amnesty, he sought to renew acquaintance with them and paid two short visits to China in 1976 and 1977. J.P. found in his father a calm acceptance of the mild joys of a simple regular life, though marred to some extent by failing health and poor hearing. He did not speak much of Fushun but he seemed happy to participate as actively as his health would allow in community and political activities centred on the provincial branch of the Chinese People's Political Consultative Conference in Kunming.

In conversations following his visits, J.P. drew a picture of his father enjoying a calm and peaceful retirement in spite of a long curtailment of freedom, and herein lay a prima facie case to consider the educational implications of a prison programme that could lead to such a seemingly happy state. This, at any rate, was the beginning of the study.

During negotiations to undertake the study, Hu Yunhong died (21 January 1978), and a request was made to the Chinese government to permit interviews of other former prisoners in his stead. The account that follows tells of how this request was met and of the consequent problems of interpretation raised.

Our first approach to the Chinese government was through its embassy in Canberra in November 1977. We summarized the purpose of our project as 'to document the reform of Hu Yunhong, former official in the Guomindang government', and we sought permission for a 40-day itinerary that would take us to Peking, Fushun and various towns in Yunnan and Jiangxi to meet members of the Hu family and to visit places of significance in Hu Yunhong's life. When the latter died we modified our project by requesting access to some other former Guomindang personnel who had undergone reform in prison. In due course we were granted a 45-day visa to visit China in January-February 1979, but without guarantee that any of our requests would be met in detail. In August 1978 I had had a preliminary discussion in Peking with Xie Li, leading member of the Chinese People's Institute of Foreign Affairs. He had assured me (though I was somewhat surprised) that access to the people and places we were seeking could quite competently be arranged by the China Travel Service. Accordingly we sought the help of a cadre from that organization when we arrived in Peking.

Zhong Qinhua of the Peking branch of the China Travel Service listened to our requests without comment and with no indication that they had already been received in writing let alone discussed before our arrival. That there must have been some prior consideration, however, is indicated by the speed with which ensuing events took place. Within two days we had begun our first round of discussions that were to last from the early afternoon of 10 January to the evening of 13 January. During these discussions, the host was Nie Zhen, Deputy Secretary-General of the fifth National Committee of the Chinese People's Political Consultative Conference, membership of which he holds as a 'specially invited personage' (*China Directory*, 1979). In the fifties, Nie had been Vice-President of the Chinese People's University where he also led a class of researchers in Marxism-Leninism (*GMRB*, 24 October 1959). He clearly retained his interest in education and at one stage during the interviews remarked that what we were learning about was 'one of the most important educational experiments in the history of mankind'. At this first round of talks, Nie introduced us to Du Yuming, Song Xilian and Huang Wei, former generals in the Guomindang army, and Pujie, former official in the Manzhouguo government and brother of last Qing Emperor, Xuan Tong (Puyi). On a later occasion we were also to meet Shen Zui, formerly of the

Guomindang Internal Security Agency. This occurred when we continued our interviews in Peking on 20 January after our return from Fushun.

The visit to Fushun, Liaoning province, was undertaken in the hope of seeing the prison which, established in 1950, was from 1956 until 1975 the main centre for the detention of high-ranking personnel. We found the prison buildings now partly occupied by ordinary prisoners. Not only were we permitted to inspect the prison and speak with its present governor, Liu Qinshi, but we were able also to interview half a dozen men who had been prison officers for some years prior to 1975. Included among these — and most importantly from the point of view of the re-education programme — was Jin Yuan, who had risen to become commandant, a position he held at the time of the last amnesty. These interviews took place on 15, 16 and 17 January. Altogether then in the period 10 January to 20 January, significant interviews took place with five ex-prisoners, six former prison officers, and Nie Zhen, representing the Chinese People's Political Consultative Conference. Later we interviewed Zhang Jingzhu and Cai Xingsan, both former senior officers of the Guomindang army, released from Fushun prison in 1975. Zhang was interviewed in Chengdu on 23 January and Cai in Hong Kong on 15 February. Talks were also had with the two deputy secretaries-general of the standing committee for Yunnan province of the Political Consultative Conference on 26 January. In addition, information has also been taken from first-hand accounts of imprisonment published by Cai Xingsan in Hong Kong and Duan Kewen in New York.

Apart from the interviews already mentioned and which provide the foundation of what follows, a considerable time was spent with members of Hu Yunhong's family in Yunnan and Jiangxi provinces, but data from these meetings will be used only incidentally in this present study.

The accounts that follow, indeed all facets of the enterprise, present a problem in interpretation. The descriptions of the prison and its routine, of the main components of reform through labour (*laodong gaizao*), the study groups, self-examinations, written confessions, criticism sessions, checking and cross-checking of facts by officials, psychological analyses, and so on are comparable, on the surface at least, with other descriptions in the literature (see bibliography). It is important to add to existing accounts these that have been collected (with one exception) from within China and with official encouragement. What is more important is to set them in context, to interpret them and to examine their implications for our understanding of the controversial practice of thought reform and any educational principles underlying it. A number of divergent interpretations can be identified. In an effort to arrive at the truth, one needs, on the one hand to avoid a too-ready acceptance of the most optimistic claims of the advocates of thought reform or even of some of its 'products' — an acceptance that would place an intolerable strain on credulity. On the other hand, one must avoid the extreme represented by an excess of scepticism that could blind one to recognition of any merit whatever even in the face of some fairly salient facts. These extreme positions can be thought to exist along several different dimensions or with respect to several viewpoints such as the leadership, the prison personnel, investigators, the world at large, prisoners themselves and, very importantly, the relationships between these different groups. An attempt is made in this study to narrow the gap between the acceptable limits of interpretation on these various dimensions. There is no single undeniable interpretation, but the study has proceeded in the belief that it is possible to set the bounds of reasonableness and within those bounds to make judgements and examine implications.

Note

1. Details of Hu Yunhong's pre-1949 career have been gathered from two main sources: (i) members of his family in Kunming and Ganzhou; (ii) an article by one of his former pupils published in Taiwan in the 1950s as one of the 'Documents on Jiangxi Province'. The writer published this article in memory of his teacher believing he had lost his life at the hands of the Communists in the spring of 1951.

2 SHEN ZUI: SECRET AGENT

'The blue-eyed boy of the late Dai Li self-willed and conceited, sly and treacherous, narrow-minded, arrogant and selfish.' These are some of the epithets used of the character Yan Zui in the novel *Hong Yan* (*Red Crag*) (Lo & Yang, 1978) written in the sixties and used as the basis for a film. Shen Zui, whom we met in Peking, claimed that the Yan Zui of the book was intended as a portrayal of himself and that it was a fairly true description. The novel's character is undoubtedly a villain, so much so that when some young friends of Shen's daughter learnt who the character Yan was supposed to represent they shuddered to think that they had been to his home.

Who was this villain in real life? Shen Zui was born in 1914 and, at the age of 18 in 1932, joined the Guomindang's internal security agency, the Bureau of Confidential Information, in the south-west district. The organization that Shen joined has appeared in a very unsavoury light to many observers, with its head, Dai Li, seen as Chiang Kai-shek's hatchet man. General Stilwell, for example, compared the Chiang regime with the Germany of Hitler: 'China, our ally, was being run by a one-party government supported by a Gestapo and headed by an unbalanced man with little education' (White, 1948: 214). Shen remained in the Guomindang's 'Gestapo' for 18 years, during which time he moved through the ranks from messenger to secret agent to section chief and, for his last six years, was director of the department of general affairs. In this last capacity he was deputy to the notorious Dai Li himself, the 'Himmler' of the regime. He reached the rank of Major-General.

Dai Li's organization had two main purposes according to Shen's account: to eliminate the Communist element and to rid the Nationalist government and the Guomindang of those who failed to support Chiang Kai-shek. The novel *Red Crag* depicts many of the cruelties by which this establishment became notorious throughout the world as well as many of the activities of the revolutionaries that the Guomindang was pledged to exterminate. There were two main sections. Besides an intelligence arm for the gathering of information there was an action section for carrying out kidnappings, assassinations and the like. Public executions were not the province of Shen's organization, but the many assassinations and kidnappings certainly were. Shen admitted to having

6

directed as many as 100 of them and was also engaged in training others to carry them out.

A particularly reprehensible event, one that horrified even many sympathizers of the Chiang government, was the killing of Professor Li Gongpu and the poet and scholar Wen Yiduo in 1946. According to the American missionary, Dr James G. Endicott (quoted in Belden, 1973: 27), Chiang ordered his 'Gestapo' to murder all twelve of a committee of scholars trying to promote a middle-way compromise government. The American and public outcry was so great when the first two assassinations became known that, according to Shen Zui, the blame was quickly shifted to a couple of scapegoats — men already under sentence of death who were now promised financial aid to their families if they would 'confess' to these new killings.

Because of the many crimes they had committed against the Communists and because they accordingly expected no mercy at their hands if caught, Shen and his colleagues continued to struggle against the Communists in south-west China for some time after the declaration of the People's Republic in 1949. They sent off their families to Hong Kong and Taiwan while they themselves remained behind to carry on the fight. When Governor Lu Han of Yunnan province eventually joined the Communist cause in December of 1949, Shen and two of his close colleagues were first detained by the government in Kunming and then handed over to the People's Liberation Army when it arrived. They fully expected to be executed, especially as, immediately prior to the liberation of Yunnan, Shen's organization had captured about 500 Communists and had made plans for their execution. The Governor's change of allegiance and the liberation of the province saved them in the nick of time.

After they had been handed over, the three agents were received by Yunnan's new Director of Public Security, Liu. Liu's courtesy and politeness took them by surprise. The Communist policy towards war criminals, he explained, was not to resort to execution or to abuse in word or deed. A free and honest confession would bring leniency, though there would be no coercion. Even so, Shen and the others imagined Liu's manner to be a subterfuge, and that, as soon as their confessions were judged complete, they would be straightway killed They developed a strategy accordingly to prolong the process as much as they could so as to extend their life.

It so happened that, although Shen Zui was quite healthy at this time, his two colleagues were not. (In fact, one of them died later while still under detention.) Their captors, recognizing their need, provided them with the best medical treatment – not merely of the kind designed to sustain life – even though medical treatment was difficult to come by at this time. When the three of them got together they would discuss whether the Communists meant business, and it was the nature of the medical services they were receiving that began to convince them that they were indeed genuine. Looking back on that period, Shen believes they were never forced to make confessions, though sometimes arguments did develop between the prisoners and their tutors. On these occasions someone from higher up would intervene to explain Communist policy. 'If you feel yourselves under pressure, this is only because the tutors become over-anxious to see you on the side of the people. You may think it is like in olden times when it was customary at the change of a dynasty for the new administration to retain some officials from the old so as to learn from them ways of oppressing the people. We assure you this is not the case now. None of your Guomindang methods will be used in our dealings with the people, so there is no way in which we are trying to learn from you. The object of your confession is your own conversion so that you too may come to serve the people.' Bit by bit then Shen and his colleagues began to tell their story to their captors, at first telling only those parts they were sure their captors would already know about.

They were not kept in Kunming for long. Apparently there was considerable local pressure, particularly from young people, for bringing them to trial and having them executed. This is the fate that many revolutionary-minded youth, for their part, had come to expect had liberation not come when it did. So the authorities, not wanting to pursue that course, judged that a calmer atmosphere would be more conducive to the re-education programme and moved the prisoners some 700km to Chongqing. This was some time in 1950 and, ironically, the prison to which they were taken had formerly been one of their own. In Chongqing and later in Peking (they were transferred there in 1956) the re-education programme was stepped up. Shen related some of the techniques and their reactions to them.

Newspapers were supplied, but Shen recalled that they did not at first want to read them. They were Communist papers and told only of production, politics and theory. In time, however, mainly through want of something better to do and to relieve boredom, they started to read, and slowly became interested, especially as they found that plans written about actually came to fruition. This seemed so unlike the former society. Through newspapers they were also introduced to the work of Chairman Mao. After a few years it was not hard to accept

Mao's writings and other Communist theory books. They began to see that Mao's policies were based on a deep understanding of the objective situation in China.

Even when Shen began to be more receptive to the idea of the new society, he still found it difficult to see himself as ever having any position in it. After all he had been one of the ruling elite in the old, and, what was more, he had close connections in Taiwan, a fact that surely would disqualify him from achieving any worthwhile status in the new society. There was, he had to agree though, no gainsaying the sincerity of the Communists.

Throughout his life, including his years in prison, Shen has kept a diary. The entries for his final year in prison, 1960, plot some of the changes that he had to undergo. He had to change his attitude towards Russia — from negative to positive, and with respect to America — from positive to negative. He had to change his view of manual labour. He had to become open in admitting the errors of the past, and he had to make all his changed positions clear. But there were some things he was not expected to change. He was able throughout to keep his personal habits: he could continue to write up his private diary, take his habitual daily cold bath and do his *taijiquan* every morning. Shen, now at the age of 65, demonstrated to us his continuing physical fitness by performing push-ups supported only by his toes and one finger of each hand. He has also retained his personal possessions, including the Rolex watch he still wears, purchased in 1948 for $US450. Shen would like to assure his compatriots in Taiwan from his own experience that Communist rule would not necessarily impose a change in an individual's personal life style.

It would be wrong to leave the impression that Shen's prison years came easily to him. He found the process of thought reform difficult. The crimes he had committed were greater and more numerous than those of generals of a great army, he said. He not only knew about torture, but he actually lectured on the subject. His status was high: his promotion to Major-General in the secret service had been more difficult than a promotion to the rank of Lieutenant-General in the army would have been. There were few such positions. Little wonder then that a man with that background and with his eye constantly on status should feel hostile towards his captors. He frequently showed his hostility, he said, by kicking up a fuss, refusing to confess, and generally trying to provoke his captors. He liked to parade this rebelliousness in front of his colleagues. As he remembers it now, this frame of mind and its accompanying behaviour persisted over some five years, during which time Public Security officers were fond of reminding him that, though a single bullet from them could finish him off, they were instead prepared to take hundreds of times that trouble to reform him. Shen on his side was confident that he would remain the exception to their reform rule.

It was expected of him by the prison authorities that he should speak his mind, though if he failed to speak out today, they would wait until tomorrow and ask again. Even when he eventually fell in with the idea of confessing, he would become depressed at his inability to recall all that he should. And depression at times led to thoughts of suicide. Because of his long experience in internal security he knew many methods of putting people to death including many ways suitable for self-destruction. However he held back from death by his own hand, preferring that his captors should kill him instead. In this way they would be accorded the blame and he would be regarded as a martyr. What Shen did not know was that he had already acquired that status. In 1953 it was reported in Taiwan that he had been killed by the Communists and his name was added to those recorded in the Martyrs' Shrine in Taipei.

Part of the technique of Shen's interrogators was to persuade him to confess details with which they were already familiar through their investigations but which he would believe they could not possibly know. An example of this was the case of the buried pistols. Just before his capture, Shen had hidden some 40 or 50 'Mauser' pistols by packing them into a coffin that he then buried, closing the tomb with a stone bearing the name 'Mauser'. Somehow or other the Communists discovered this little act and exhumed the coffin and its contents. Painstakingly the story was teased out of Shen, with no let-up until every detail was clear. When he could not remember the precise number of pistols he had concealed, this failure of his memory caused him considerable anxiety.

He also became anxious over his inability to recall the many cases of espionage he had engineered either by sending a Guomindang agent into the Communist ranks or by converting a Communist to the Guomindang cause. He thought at the time that the authorities were quite unreasonable in pressing him to remember and confess in such detail.

Besides items he could not remember, there were those he dared not reveal. For instance, he did not disclose, until long after his release (in fact not until after the downfall of the Gang of Four) what he knew about Zhang Chunqiao, one of the Gang. Shen's information was that Zhang was a secret Guomindang agent planted in the ranks of the

the Communists, having established himself there by using typical Guomindang tricks. This is information he was not willing to part with at the time for fear of reprisals from Zhang himself, occupant still of a not insignificant position within the Communist Party machine. At this point in the discussion, Shen interpolated some derogatory comments about features of the Gang's decade of power from the beginning of the Cultural Revolution. In some ways, he thought, the Gang's behaviour was worse than that of pre-Liberation Guomindang. At least the Guomindang had been sensitive to world opinion and to the reactions of the people at large, a sensitivity evidenced by their attempted cover-up of the assassination of Li Gongpu and Wen Yiduo. The Gang never displayed any such reservation.

Reflecting on the secrets of the Communists' success in reforming their enemies, Shen pointed to the fact that, with all their patient if dogged persistence, they never demeaned one. A person's integrity was always respected. Argument was carried on with reason, and debate was permitted. The prisoners were in fact often far more agitated in argument than the officers. No one was coerced to say or do other than through his own will and conviction. And just as their personality was protected, so also was their body looked after well. The prisoners were provided with better food than were the cadres themselves. It is clear that the authorities were keeping in mind the former 'good' life to which their charges had been accustomed. The prisoners were often embarrassed into requesting a reduction in their diet, but the leadership always argued that they should accept what they had become used to.

Even now, years after release, that favoured treatment continues. At more than ¥100 a month, Shen's present salary is higher than that of some cadres. He has a good position as the senior member of the Committee on Documents and Literature of the National Committee of the People's Political Consultative Conference. As such he has the chance of writing the history of the current generation, not leaving that task to the next generation as has been the custom in the past. Shen is writing about the relationship between the Guomindang and the Communist Party, particularly about some of the Guomindang's more secret intentions, including a number of undercover methods aimed at the downfall of the Communists. He is focussing on the political struggle rather than the military.

Shen appears to harbour no regrets over his reformation and he told his story with enthusiasm and good humour. His release from prison came when he was pardoned in November 1960. His close colleague, Zhou Yanghao, was not, however, set free until nearly 15 years later. Shen attributes the fact that Zhou was kept so long to his stubbornness in refusing to make a clean breast of his crimes. He repeatedly baulked at acknowledging his culpability on the grounds that the many killings he had carried out had been done under orders. One of these killings may well have been the secret execution of General Yang Hucheng of the Nationalist 17th Route Army. Yang, with the 'Young' Marshall Zhang Xueliang, had been closely implicated in the Xi'an kidnapping of Chiang Kai-shek in 1936. According to Shen Zui, Zhou Yanghao was in charge of the Xifeng concentration camp in Guizhou province to which Yang Hucheng had been sent following a period of detention in Chongqing. It is clear that Chiang Kai-shek never forgave either Zhang or Yang. Zhang Xueliang remained his personal prisoner in Taiwan for the rest of the Generalissimo's life; Yang failed to emerge alive from Zhou Yanghao's concentration camp. At the end of 1967, Zhou was transferred (along, incidentally, with General Huang Wei) from Peking to the Fushun prison where his re-education was continued for the next seven years. Shen doubts whether, even then, Zhou's reformation would have been complete. He was one of the ten who, on release, elected to go to Taiwan. He had hoped to join his family there, but the authorities would not admit him. He settled instead in America.

There is no more than a fine line between fame and notoriety. A change of audience is sufficient to convert one to the other, and for some people who seek the limelight the distinction is of minor importance. It satisfies Shen Zui's conceit now to relish a notoriety that derives from what he was at pains to paint as a one-time awesome reputation, albeit restricted to a few observers because of the nature of the activities on which it was based. His self-esteem came through in a number of ways during interviews. He took care in his account to emphasize his status both in the former Guomindang organization and as a current member of the People's Political Consultative Conference at the national level. He delighted in telling ancedotes of his cleverness. At a more personal level he was unreserved in displaying his physical prowess, and, like a proud schoolboy, enjoyed being flattered on the neatness and detail of his personal diary. To his present notoriety, which can afford a far wider audience than was desirable with the fame from which it derives, add the opportunity to speak to posterity as a contemporary historian, and there is a situation with which a person of Shen's ego must be well satisfied.

3 DU YUMING: INCOMPETENT GENERAL, WILLING PUPIL

> You are now at the end of your rope ... You should ...
> immediately order all your troops to lay down their arms and
> cease resistance ... If you still want to fight another round,
> you can have it, but you will be finished off anyway.
> (Message broadcast to Du Yuming and others by Mao Zedong
> on 17 December 1948 (Mao, *SW*, IV: 295-6))

Another round was fought and Du Yuming, Deputy Commander-in-Chief of the Guomindang's Xuzhou Bandit Suppression Headquarters, fell captive to the Communists' Third Field Army commanded by Chen Yi, so concluding, simultaneously, on 10 January 1949, one of the largest campaigns in military history — the Huai-Hai campaign — and Du's inglorious military career. As a Field Marshall in Chiang Kai-shek's army, Du Yuming had been one of the first to engage the Communists in battle after the Sino-Japanese war. From then on he proceeded to lose every one of his battles throughout the ensuing three or four years of fighting. When we met him 30 years after his defeat, he was a Shanghai deputy to the fifth National People's Congress and a member of the presidium of the National Committee in Peking of the Chinese People's Political Consultative Conference. To link these two states is to draw closer to understanding the Chinese Communists' plan of re-educating their former enemies.

The Communists set about wooing Du from the moment of his capture and it appears that they found him a not unwilling subject, by and large.

Immediately following his defeat he was attached to Commander Chen Yi's headquarters in Jinan, Shandong province. Here we find him enjoying the Commander's hospitality at a dinner party and having conversations with a former Whampoa colleague, General Chang, who had earlier forsaken the Nationalist army for the Communist cause. He declares that he soon began to perceive fundamental differences between the People's Liberation Army and his own army and started being interested enough to read some revolutionary novels and to commence a study of some of the writings of Mao Zedong. In particular he remembers reading at this time *On Practice*. It is in this essay that Mao, in 1937, struck out at the twin evils (as he saw them) of dogmatism

13

and empiricism, both ineffective in producing the revolutionary change necessary to improve the world. 'And the objective world which is to be changed also includes all the opponents of change who, in order to be changed, must go through a stage of compulsion before they can enter the stage of voluntary, conscious change' (Mao, *SW* I: 295-309).

It was to be almost a decade before Du's stage of compulsion was formally concluded, although during this period he had considerably more freedom than must have been the case of many prisoners of war. Certainly he spoke approvingly of his treatment while under detention. He recalled with much amusement the special meals prepared for him when he was transferred to the protection of a People's Liberation Army corps in Peking. He was a general, so naturally he must be served 'big grain' (rice) especially prepared rather than 'small grain' (millet), the more common staple cooked in bulk. Although he could recognize the respect intended, his upbringing in Shanxi province dictated a personal preference for the latter, and (he laughs about it now) he would try to exchange dishes with some of the ordinary soldiers.

One way to help win over a person is to ask his advice and this was a tactic put to good use by the Communist rulers in respect of Du Yuming. With the outbreak of the Korean war in 1950, Du, having formerly been in collaboration with the United States, was asked for his evaluation of the American forces. As he was now beginning to see things in a new light he was quite happy to accede to this request. He had previously misconstrued the nature of patriotism, he said, but now realized that the Guomindang government had been working, not for the general good of the country he loved, but for the benefit of capitalism and in particular for the Four Families, the families of Chiang Kai-shek, Chen Lifu, H.H. Kung and T.V. Soong. Along with this realization about patriotism dawned an understanding of the true nature of war and why it was that the Guomindang with modern weapons had lost to the People's Liberation Army who were fighting a people's war.

With the two problems of war and patriotism mastered, it became an easy step to acknowledge his past crime and to decide how he wanted to plan the future. Du sets this period of realization and eventual confession at about six or seven years, during most of which time he was held in the Peking War Criminals Administration Centre. Here he participated in regular study sessions, self-examinations and recreational activities. He claims that never during this time was a confession to any past wrongs demanded of him, but he began to reflect and to contrast the new society with the old. Still, he had some reservations about what the Communists were doing, he said. What eventually helped him to an appreciation of the line they were taking and of the correctness of Mao Zedong Thought were the tours arranged towards the end of the fifties to show him developments in the new society.

Perhaps the most difficult concept he had to grapple with was that of the class struggle and the notion that a deliberate effort to extinguish a class does not entail the extinction of the people of that class, only their re-education. Had this been clear to him at the outset he would not have been so surprised at not being executed on capture but would have understood how it was that people privileged in the old society (as he was) were still to be cared for in the new.

Du certainly had been cared for by his own account. In his days as a general under the Guomindang his health had been bad — like that of a number of other Guomindang leaders. He had been suffering from kidney, lung and spinal trouble and needed a stick to help him walk. In the hands of the Communists, his ailments were properly diagnosed and treated and he was nursed to recovery. His life became more energetic and more meaningful and he began to take part in manual work, sewing his own clothing and joining in tree-planting.

Such, in substance, was the account that Du offered as his story, delivered in a strong deliberate voice. If the People's Republic's treatment of war criminals is more like schooling than punishment, then Du must be near the top of the class. He was held up as a model by Xie Juezai in the same address as quoted from at the beginning of this book, and former war prisoner Cai Xingsan, though not sharing the same prison as Du, has passed on reports from those who were with him in Peking. 'Among the political prisoners in Peking, Du Yuming was regarded as very good. It was said that he admitted all his mistakes and he studied seriously. He wrote his notes neatly and well, especially the articles he submitted to the cadres which he wrote in formal script. He even made notes on Mao Zedong's article "On Protracted Warfare". He also made a request to send this article of Mao to President Chiang in Taiwan.'

Taiwan. Because of his changed views and because of his family ties with Taiwan, Du has been one of those former Guomindang members who have tried to influence policy there. This came to light during a session in which we addressed some specific questions to Du. The answers to these questions are recorded verbatim.

Q. How did you come to be released relatively soon?
I do not know fully why the authorities released me, but I did arrive at an understanding of the truth: I began to understand theories of the class struggle and liberation by the proletariat according to the theories of Marx.

Q. When did you begin to acquire hope of release?
On 10 January 1956, seven years to the day when I was taken prisoner. On that day it was announced in study sessions that, according to Party policy, reform education would be intensified so that prisoners could work with the hope of more liberal treatment. Throughout my stay in prison I became convinced that the Communist Party never tells lies, always honours its every promise.

Q. What were some of the memorable events during your imprisonment?
I shall name three:
1. the recovery of my health;
2. a realization of the significance of class struggle;
3. seeing the increase in production since Nationalist days.

Q. Can you tell us something about your family?
I came from the family of a small landlord. My father had been a successful candidate in the imperial examinations, attaining the grade of *juren*, and had become a member of Sun Yat-sen's political party. Thus I was exposed to Sun's *Three Principles of the People* (*San min zhuyi:* Nationalism, People's democracy, People's livelihood) from an early age.

   One of my daughters is married in the USA to the 1957 Nobel Prize winning physicist, Yang Zhenning.[1] When Yang went to Helsinki to receive the Nobel Prize in 1957, I managed through the authorities to ask the Chinese delegate to take a letter to him. In this way I was able to get in touch with my daughter who then contacted my wife in Taiwan saying that 'an old friend' had informed her that I was alive. Of course she would know that the 'old friend' was none other than myself. At this same time, the Taiwan government granted Yang the highest science honour, making him a member of the Science Academy. Yang's parents resided in China, but the American government would not allow him to visit them there. He used to meet them from time to time in Hong Kong. Mme Chiang Kai-shek received my wife and gave her travelling expenses to go to America with a view to persuading Yang to settle in Taiwan. She told Mme Chiang that she would rather have advised him not to go to Taiwan. She herself was planning to return to China.

My wife returned to China in June 1963 (having been in the USA since the spring of 1958). During this period (1958-63) she kept in touch with me. Her manner of returning was interesting. She flew from the United States to Geneva on her Taiwan passport and then, with the help of the People's Republic, she flew from there to China. I met her at the airport along with a number of government officials. My wife is still here in Peking, where she and I are looked after by a maid.

The Chiang regime has restricted my children in Taiwan from leaving there. Apart from my daughter in America, I have, in Taiwan, two sons, two daughters, and six grandchildren. As re-unification comes closer, the prospect of my seeing my children becomes brighter. Incidentally, after my release, I made a number of broadcasts to Taiwan telling of conditions here.

Q. What have been your main activities since 1960?
I have been writing my memoirs. They have been mostly accounts and evaluations of battles and have had a limited publication. They should prove valuable to future historians. None of them relates to my imprisonment, though I did write during that period. Those writings are not in my possession.

Q. What is the major message you would like conveyed to the rest of the world?
Marxism and Mao Zedong Thought provide the basic principles for reforming the world. Socialism is the only way to save China, and I would like to think of my offspring in the future carrying the socialist banner.

Note

1. Yang had an audience with Mao Zedong in 1973, and in 1977 he met both Hua Guofeng and Deng Xiaoping in Peking. Born in Anhui province he graduated from the National Southwest Associated University in Kunming, and then took a scholarship to study in Chicago in 1945. He is now the Albert Einstein professor and director of the Institute for Theoretical Physics of the State University of New York.

4 SONG XILIAN: ALWAYS A PATRIOT

Mao-like in appearance, plump, round-faced and comfortable, Song Xilian, now in his seventy-third year, looked at ease in his armchair and, eyes half-closed beneath a common blue peaked cap, seemed scarcely aware of conversations around him. Addressed directly though, he would come to life, eyes twinkling with a gentle all-encompassing smile.

Perhaps the sad thing about Song's ten year imprisonment is that it should have befallen one so in love with his country and whose important life decisions were motivated by this love. It was a patriotism that began early. From 1921 when he was 14, Song studied in Changsha and there became interested in movements for reform, just as had Mao Zedong ten years earlier in the same city. Like Mao too, he wanted to become a soldier, so it seemed providential that, just as he came to the end of his schooldays, he heard of the establishment in the suburbs of Canton of the Whampoa Military Academy. Set up by the Nationalist Party with the collaboration of the Communist Party, and sponsored and supplied in money and staff by Soviet Russia anxious to promote a new China, the Academy seemed to offer the young Song just the opportunity he was seeking to serve his country. It was Sun Yat-sen's Guomindang policy at this time (brief as it turned out) to ally with the Soviet Union and accept members of the Communist Party. All seemed set therefore for a united assault on the sickness afflicting a divided China. Song applied for entry and was accepted as one of the Academy's first students. He recalls that, such were the difficulties of travel at the time, that in order to reach Canton from Changsha (today a rail journey of 740km) he had first to go north to Wuhan and then pursue his way by river and sea through Shanghai and Hong Kong, an impressive excursion of nearly 3000km. At the Academy Song came under the influence both of Chiang Kai-shek as military director and of Zhou Enlai as the cadets' political educator. He was sufficiently impressed by Zhou's teaching to become a member like Zhou of the Communist Party in 1925; but it was Chiang Kai-shek and the Guomindang rather than the Communists that were to claim his effective allegiance for the next two decades. The army of the newly reorganized Guomindang was in pressing need of trained personnel, so the course of training for some of the Academy's early cadets was short indeed. Song's period lasted only from May to September 1924 after which he found himself to be a commissioned officer.

Before long he was commanding a battalion in the twenty-first division of the National Revolutionary Army. His erstwhile military teacher, Chiang, was now Commander-in-Chief of all the armed forces, having been appointed to that position in mid-1926, the express purpose of the Guomindang being that he should wrest China from the power of the northern warlords and bring about a measure of unity to the nation. Song threw himself with youthful vigour into what became known as the Northern Expedition. He assisted in the occupation of Wuhan and the seizure of the British concession in Hankou in October 1926. Then, with his troops, he turned eastwards down the valley of the Yangtze reaching Nanjing by the following March. When later he arrived at Shanghai, he was injured badly enough in the fighting to be put into hospital and to be relieved temporarily of his army post. In the circumstances this may have been a fortunate escape for Song, for it was about this time — April 1927 — that Chiang instigated his purge of Communists from the Guomindang. By the time Song was fit again he had (as he expressed it in interview) 'lost touch' with the Communist Party.

In tracing a person's life there is some fascination in identifying, with hindsight, the major decision points along the way. Song's decision after recovering his health must surely rate as one of these. At a loose end, he sought to rejoin the Nationalist army. He wrote to Chiang who responded immediately with a proposal that seemed to offer him splendid prospects. He was to leave forthwith for Japan to embark on a three-year study of military science. This proposal he eagerly accepted and, in so doing, determined his future for a number of years to come. Throughout the thirties and early forties he held various posts fighting in the civil war and in the Sino-Japanese war.

By 1946 he held the highest military command in Xinjiang province, and in August 1948 he was transferred to Wuhan as Deputy Field-Marshall of the central plains area and commander of the 7th Army Corps. An almost impossible task now confronted him. This new call on his services was part of Chiang's desperate attempt to hold on to the Yangtze valley, and, to do this, Song and his fellow officers had to reconstitute an army that had, in Hubei and northern Hunan, suffered devastating defeats at the hands of the Communists under Chen Yi and Lin Biao. The Communists by now had passed from guerrilla to large-scale positional warfare and in so doing had rendered themselves clear and plausible contenders for a rival government. From now on the three great campaigns of Liaoxi-Shenyang September to November 1948, Huai river-Longhai railway November 1948, and Beiping-Tianjin January 1949 (referred to in the two-character portmanteau fashion of the Chinese as the Liao-Shen, Huai-Hai and Ping-Jin) were all but to wipe out the Nationalist forces north of the Yangtze, clearing the way for the declaration in Peking of the People's Republic. For a time from October 1949 onwards, the south and west remained under Guomindang control, with Song in military charge of the region. But this was not be be for long. December 1949 found him fleeing with 10,000 men before a Communist advance led by Liu Bocheng, the 'one-eyed Dragon', who had none other than Deng Xiaoping for his political commissar. During this advance, Song was taken prisoner by the commander of the Communists' 5th Army Corps, Yang Yong. (At the time of writing, Yang Yong is currently a Deputy Chief of Staff of the PLA, having formerly been military commander of Xinjiang province.)

Song says now that he thought being captured would mean certain execution and in his mind he prepared himself for death. One of the formalities after his capture was that he should be photographed. His unwillingness to submit to what seemed to him an unnecessary piece of red tape angered the photographer who deplored that he had not a gun rather than a camera. Song's retort was that he had been expecting a gun and was quite ready for it. Evidently the photographer reported the incident higher up, for shortly afterwards General Yang called Song in to explain Chairman Mao's very different policy on prisoners of war, which was not to kill but to reform.

After a short stay in the regional centre Leshan, Song was sent to the Chongqing war prisoners' camp, where he stayed for about four years along with a number of other former high-ranking officers. (Shen Zui was also imprisoned here. See Chapter 2.) During his stay in Chongqing, he received a number of day-long visits from a fellow provincial, a former schoolmate in fact, who was now a member of the People's Liberation Army. Their conversations started him thinking again about Communism and he set about buying for himself a number of books on Marxism and Leninism and some of the published pamphlets of Mao Zedong's writings and speeches. He remembers being especially impressed by the article 'On New Democracy' (Mao, *SW*, II: 339-84) published in Yan'an in 1940 and by the report to the Seventh National Congress of the Communist Party on China (April 1945), 'On Coalition Government' (Mao, *SW*, III: 205-70). This latter, in part Mao's answer to Chiang's *China's Destiny* published in 1943, sets forth

China's other destiny and, for Song, must have amounted to a reformulation of the choice with which he had been confronted in his days as a young graduate from the Whampoa Academy. Here he was again at a decision point borne upon him now by circumstances more forcible than before. Yet, he recalled, he still had reservations about the Communist vision for China.

Some of these reservations began to fade in the light of the tangible achievements of the People's Republic in its first few years: the curbing of inflation, the completion of the Chengdu-Chongqing railway (talked about for years before 1948), the entry into the Korean war in 1950 on a matter of principle even though there was so much to be done at home.

In 1955, after four years at Chongqing, Song was moved to Peking. In the Peking prison, prisoners were expected to take greater responsibility for their own education and for their daily routine than at Chongqing where they were 'looked after' by the authorities. They were organized into groups that combined study and day-to-day routine functions. Song, for instance, was leader of a large group made up of ten smaller groups each comprising twelve members. (He had been a small group leader in Chongqing for three years.) The prime purpose of the group was study, but it was also geared to routine matters such as registering hospital patients and issuing supplies.

Except on Sundays, there were four hours of study per day. The study had two aspects. In theory they examined the works of Marx, Lenin and Chairman Mao. In current affairs they kept up with mass movements and other events through reading newspapers and magazines. They had both broad and penetrating discussions and argument was encouraged. Song does recall, however, that they were apt to encounter criticism if they waged argument against the fundamental policies of the Communist Party.

All prisoners were expected to write reports. A short report was to be written each week and a longer one annually. The annual evaluation would be read out to the rest of the group who were then able to raise questions for amplification. Staff members were often present at these readings.

The main content of the annual evaluation related to the individual's findings about his own thoughts, how he had improved, what doubts he still had. He would give a brief account of his life in the year just past, problems still unsolved and plans for the coming year. The completed report was handed to the authorities. Song imagines that the authorities took some notice of these reports, but he is unable to be certain of this.

There were occasional individual sessions with someone in authority, and sometimes it was the large group of 120 that was used to counter reactionary behaviour on the part of the individual. Song recounted two cases of large-scale meetings. One was on behalf of a prisoner Zhang who believed it possible for a compromise between the classes in society. It took two general meetings to deal with his heresy. The other was the case of former general Huang Wei (cf. Chapter 5) who, for a long time, showed no interest whatever in study, preferring instead to spend his time inventing a perpetual motion machine. He had continued thus in spite of a pronouncement from scientists at the Chinese Academy of Sciences that the design was an impossible one. The large group was mobilized to help and criticize Huang for indulging in impossible pursuits when he ought to have been concerned with his own thought reform. The group also sought the help of Huang's wife from Shanghai and of his daughter at Qinghua University in an effort to dissuade him from his unfounded ideas. That was in 1956-7. Huang withstood all such efforts and Song expressed the definite opinion that therein lies the reason that Huang's release from prison did not come until 16 years after that of his colleagues.

Song's own release came in 1959. As early as 1956 he was given hope that he might soon be set free. China at that time was experiencing a general air of tolerance, the period of the Hundred Flowers movement. As a preparation for their re-entry into society and as a rounding-off of their re-education programme, the prisoners were taken on tours to various places to see developments. They went, for example, to visit the Anshan steel mill, severely damaged in 1945 during the Japanese war, and now impressively restored. Song was also impressed by the new bridge at Wuhan. During these tours, the prisoners were fairly free to move around by themselves, and they were struck not only by material reconstruction but also by the absence of social ills like prostitution and begging. Before Song's anticipated early release eventuated however, there was a change of climate, the Anti-rightist campaign swung into action to counter the excesses of the Hundred Flowers and the prison doors that had begun to open were once more double locked. The decision of the Standing Committee of the National People's Congress on the first special amnesty had to wait until 17 September 1959. It was promulgated the same day, and the actual release occurred on 4 December of the same year.

When asked about the most significant and memorable aspect to be recollected from his imprisonment, Song spoke of his new respect for life. As a career soldier he had tended to ignore the value that might reside in life itself. He had put the problem of life and death to one side. He has now, thanks to the staff members in prison, a new outlook. The starting point of his reform was the realization that it was not Communist policy to kill but to treat life with respect. He was never insulted by prison officers. Educate, not abuse, was their watchword and their educational approach was encouragement rather than enforcement.

In 1978 the National Committee of the People's Political Consultative Conference arranged a tour for former prisoners, in the course of which there was a visit to Chongqing. Here Song felt his new respect for life well up within him, and, remembering that Chongqing was where Chiang Kai-shek, his former chief, had ordered the killing of some 300 or 400 Communists or suspected Communists merely on political grounds, he was moved to write a poem.

Song is contented in his advancing years. He lives in Peking with his second wife and her daughter. His first wife, whom he married in 1933, died in June 1949 leaving two sons and three daughters ranging in age from eight to 16. These were cared for by an aunt first in Hong Kong then in Taiwan. They now live in the United States of America. The eldest son, a musician, has visited his father twice in recent years.

Song believes that all truth is relative, but one thing is certain for him. The new China is undoubtedly better than the old, and only the Chinese Communist Party had been able to bring about this improvement. Convinced of that, he is happy to support the present regime. He is a Standing Committee member of the fifth National Committee of the People's Political Consultative Conference. A Nationalist at heart, Song Xilian has throughout his life based his decisions on patriotism, though his analysis of the situation has not always led him to side with the forces of history in his application of this most worthy sentiment. Now after a long journey he has arrived.

5   HUANG WEI: AMATEUR SCIENTIST

> I will show you him that was a lion until then, and is now
> a lamb.
>
> (J. Wesley, *Journal*, vol. II.)

Huang Wei, former Lieutenant-General and commander of the
Guomindang 12th army, was one of Chiang Kai-shek's most loyal
officers. His capture at the climax of the decisive Huai-Hai battle in
December 1948 signalled the demise of the once powerful Nationalist
Central Army and the certain success of the Communist forces. More
than 26 years later, the victorious Communists still sought to draw
profit from Huang as they thrust him with his family into the full
glare of the publicity flooding the 1975 amnesty. The press for both
home and foreign readers carried the story, with pictures, of his
address of thanks on behalf of the 293 Guomindang prisoners granted
their pardon. 'I am infinitely encouraged, elated and grateful', he is
reported as having said in part. 'I resolve to continue moving over to
the people's side, making a new man of myself and doing my part to
build socialism and liberate Taiwan' (*CR*, XXIV(7): 14). He was 72
years old.

Throughout much of the 26-year period between capture and
release, Huang steadfastly resisted attempts at thought reform, focusing
his mind instead on a seemingly impossible dream — the design of a
perpetual motion machine. Most of his would-be converters rated him
as inherently and incurably obstinate: it took Jin Yuan of Fushun, into
whose charge he came late in his imprisonment, to understand Huang's
ploy and to match it. He could see that Huang was acting, perhaps
unawares, on the proposition that one is less likely to succumb to an
attack on one's integrity by maintaining a policy of complete non-
co-operation than by attempting a display of strength and courage
in argument. 'Whoever refuses to co-operate in any technique of
conversion or brain-washing and, instead of paying attention to the
interrogator or preacher, manages to concentrate mentally on some
quite different problem, should last out the longest' (Sargant, 1957:
226). Rudyard Kipling's Kim, Sargant reminds us, resisted hypnosis by
recalling multiplication tables. Huang Wei resisted reform by puzzling
over perpetual motion.

We knew nothing of Huang's technological interests when we first met him in Peking in the company of Nie Zhen and of former prisoners, Du Yuming, Song Xilian and Pujie, and even then it was not from Huang himself we learnt the story. First mention came from Song Xilian who was convinced that it was an interest in mechanical invention that kept Huang imprisoned for 16 years longer than he himself. We learnt something of the matter also from Huang's two daughters. The prison personnel in Fushun then gave their version and, more recently, Huang's former co-prisoner, Cai Xingsan, has published an account in Hong Kong. Since leaving prison, Huang has continued to develop his idea to the point where a paper he wrote in 1979 has received serious attention in Peking. That this chapter in Huang's life is not closed even today reflects the persistence and strength of will of the man. It also illuminates some aspects of the way the re-education policy was administered in the Fushun prison. But before embarking here on the tale of the perpetual motion machine, it is desirable to sketch Huang's background and pass on his own account of his prison days.

It was a day and a half before he uttered more than the customary courtesies. While others began their story, he sat back in his armchair surveying the scene with a supercilious air that was accentuated by a curled upper lip. I remember expecting, fascinated as I was by the old soldier's face, that when he did decide it was incumbent upon him to begin his account we should probably hear very little from him. I was wrong. Taking the floor, as it were, on the afternoon of the second day, and holding our interest for the better part of the next day too, he delivered his life story with unexpected verve and emotion.

He re-lived his battles, felt again his once unswerving loyalty to Chiang Kai-shek, suffered yet again the ignominy of a crushing defeat, remembered with tenderness the devotion of his late wife, and became excited as he recalled for us the stubbornness with which he resisted reform. Parts of his recital were repetitious, but what was lacking in precision was made good in forthrightness and liveliness. In his thick Jiangxi accents he commanded his audience — and this included Nie Zhen who listened as attentively as if he had known none of it before.

Huang was brought up in Jiangxi province in the comfortable circumstances of a family owning land from which it drew rent. He attended normal school from which he graduated to become a primary school teacher. He soon realized however that he was totally unsuited for teaching. Restless, ambitious and impatient, he looked about for something with more of a challenge. And challenge there was to young people of spirit and talent if they were tuned into any of the patriotic and nationalistic debates and movements of the early twenties. When Huang heard of Sun Yat-sen's call to help raise the banner against the warlords, this seemed to present the opportunity that Huang was looking for. The warlords, he believed, were destructive of China's unity and prosperity. He had first-hand experience of this in his home province, for Jiangxi was one of several eastern provinces still largely controlled by foreign-backed Sun Chuanfang, and when Huang decided to try for entry to the newly established Whampoa Military Academy in Canton, he had therefore to keep his intention to himself. He journeyed to Shanghai (also under the same warlord's control), where he was able to gain preliminary but secret assurance of a place in the Academy, and finally to Canton where he gained free admission along with Du Yuming and Song Xilian. He was happy as he embarked on this path, happy to be a follower of Sun Yat-sen and a believer in the Three Principles of the People which, if put into practice, would restore dignity to China and deliver power to the Chinese people at large.

At the Academy Huang of course came into contact with future Communist premier, Zhou Enlai, who was a political commissar there, but he did not think that Soviet-model Communism was the answer to China's problems.

After commanding a battalion in the Northern Expedition of 1926 under Commander-in-Chief Chiang Kai-shek, Huang was selected for further training at the high prestige Military Staff College (Lujun daxuexiao) in Nanjing. Huang must have been a model product of Luda and it is impressive to observe in him today the qualities it then promoted. Not only was the college geared to teaching military science, but its educational policy, drawn up by the Generalissimo himself as its ex-officio President, was marked by a strong ethical vein.

> Special emphasis must be given to ethical training, for leadership through moral inspiration is indispensable to high commanders and important staff officers. Great attention, therefore, must be directed to inculcating, besides the necessary military knowledge and techniques, military morality and martial spirit . . . The educational concept of the college is centred in the shaping of fine and persevering qualities in the students' personalities; to develop in them the attributes of virtuous citizenship and soldierly spirit and to harmonize these with scientific knowledge of military principles, of the skill of command, and the procedures of war. It aims to bring forth the students' instinctive ability to face exigency, the power of comprehending military principles, the art of applying these

principles in practice, and the ability to handle administrative affairs. The fundamental approach lies in the students' correct understanding of the meaning of *responsibility*; their appreciation of initiative, flexibility, and speedy decisiveness; their obstinate spiritual courage; their broad comprehension of the situation confronting them, and their constructiveness in applying their knowledge.

(*Lujun daxuexiao jiaoyu kanling* (The Educational Policy of the Army Staff College), Nanjing, 1930. Quoted in Liu (1956): 85)

Huang took these aims seriously and became known in time as one of Chiang Kai-shek's most loyal senior officers. His 'obstinate spiritual courage' no doubt sustained him in battle: it also kept him in prison long after some of his close colleagues were released.

Following his studies at Luda, Huang was promoted to a commission in his native province of Jiangxi, which had been wrested from the control of warlord Sun Chuanfang during the Northern Expedition. By this time though there was open breach between the Guomindang and the Communist Party and the Nationalists were determined to wipe out the Communists' Soviet experiment centred on Ruijin in southeast Jiangxi. Huang Wei there became personally involved as a divisional commander in the encirclement campaigns against the Communists. He recalled for us that his division, the 11th, suffered considerable loss in the fourth encirclement, but that he also took part in the successful fifth of 1933-4 which triggered off the famous Long March of the Communists.

There followed three years during which Huang was very busy in the training of others. He taught at the Central Military Academy (moved by then from Canton to the Nationalist capital, Nanjing). He took charge for a time of the training department in the Academy of Military Science stationed in Guilin, an infantry training centre offering short intensive courses for men withdrawn from the front. He also established a new academy at Wuhan after the American model. He pointed out that this wide experience meant that he has been trainer or superior officer to some of Taiwan's present highest military commanders. He has offered to go to Taiwan to talk to these officers as a step towards the normalizing of relations between the two governments, but Taiwan has so far not responded to the proposal.

There had been a marked German flavour in the curriculum and ethos of the Staff College and Huang was set to have this influence strengthened several years after his graduation and following the experience both in action and in teaching that has just been described. He was chosen to take up advanced studies in military science in Germany itself. He embarked in February 1937, but it was to be an all too brief excursion. He was recalled within six months because of the renewed Japanese threat occasioned by the Marco Polo Bridge incident of 7 July. Huang recollected that the actual date of his arrival home, 13 August, coincided with the bloody confrontation in Shanghai that marked the beginning of the Sino-Japanese war in eastern China. He immediately took command of the 67th division of the 18th Army Corps, stationed on the right bank of the Yangtze river.

During the Sino-Japanese war, Huang saw a good deal of action in the Shanghai area. The Chinese fought a number of battles of heroic proportions against the Japanese and the losses were huge. In Huang's opinion, to defend Shanghai was a poor decision on the part of Chiang and he became very agitated as he thought about it. Looking back now, he believed that Chiang did not know how to mobilize the people. His chief interest lay in winning the commendation of international allies fully expecting thereby that international intervention would end the conflict. As it was, the losses were too great. Most of China's crack forces were crushed and there was no presentable fighting after that.

Following the withdrawal from Shanghai, Huang retreated with his troops to the south of Anhui province to assist in the defence of Nanjing, though he did not penetrate beyond the periphery of the fighting before that city fell on 12 December 1937. A month before, the seat of government had been moved from Nanjing to Wuhan and it was towards this centre that the Japanese next directed their thrust. Huang went to the defence of Wuhan (which fell to the Japanese in October 1938), but he said little about this except to repeat his view that the Chinese army was too weakened after Shanghai-Nanjing to put up any respectable fight against the enemy.

Huang's narrative took a leap at this point to 1948. By that time the Communists had extended their political influence throughout many parts of the country, and the tension that had been building up steadily between the two Chinese parties during the Sino-Japanese war had erupted into armed conflict after the end of the Pacific War and Japan's surrender into the hands of the Allied Powers. The creation of the People's Liberation Army had been announced in 1946 and, by 1948, having acquired the upper hand in the north-east, was set to descend on the strategic Xuzhou area between the Yellow and the Yangtze rivers. Huang took up his story at the point when, in September 1948, he assumed command of the 12th army corps, a combination of the 18th, 10th, 14th and 85th armies, and set off towards Xuzhou. Marching eastward from southern Henan and northern Hubei, weighed down with heavy United States equipment, and impeded by mud and snow and small battles on the way, they found the going slow and difficult. There was poor communication or none at all between the various commanders and what communication network did exist was infiltrated by the Communists. In fact, from the beginning the initiative lay with the Communist forces and Huang's army group found itself encircled by them at Shuangduiji, some 100km south-west of Xuzhou.

Huang became very agitated as he told of his part in the battles of this Huai-Hai campaign. There were four Nationalist Army Corps, he said, with 500,000 soldiers. The People's Liberation Army first concentrated on defeating the 7th Army Corps under the command of Huang Botao. General Huang Botao was killed in action and his corps annihilated. The Communists then turned their attention to the defeat of Huang Wei's 12th Army Corps. The Communist strength was five times that of Huang Wei's and the latter's troops were incapable of defence for want of supplies and food rations. By the 15 December they could resist no more. Chiang Kai-shek asked General Du Yuming to go to the relief of Huang Wei, but he, too, was powerless in the face of the opposition. Nor were Generals Li Yannian and Liu Ruming any more successful from the Bengbu direction.

In the last few days of 1948, when Huang's forces were pressed to the limit, Chiang guaranteed to use the whole air force to cover their withdrawal. He even sanctioned the use of poison gas and dropped the necessary equipment for this from the air. So highly did Chiang cherish the loyalty of Huang and his troops that he was determined to save them at all costs. Huang Wei said that he did in fact give the order to use the poison gas (admittedly on a small scale) even though he knew he was thereby transgressing an international convention.

Huang tried to escape in a tank, but the liberation forces were everywhere, even 50 or 60km away from the battle centre. He was captured at Suxian. His deputy commander, General Hu Lian, managed to escape with an entire division, and this division became the nucleus of the new 12th Army Corps which evacuated to Quemoy at the end of 1949, thus ensuring that Quemoy remained in Guomindang hands. That same commander, Hu, was still there at the time of the 1958 bombardment, Huang added.

After his capture, because he had inflicted great losses on the Communists both in the thirties and during the Huai-Hai campaign, Huang thought there could be no way that he would be permitted to live. In the face of what seemed to him the prospect of certain death he felt remarkably resigned and at peace. But there was no mention of execution and, in fact, he was well treated. Still he had no intention of co-operating with his captors, and when they asked him to write or broadcast a surrender appeal to General Du Yuming he refused.

Still loyal to Chiang he was prepared to die for him. It was obvious that he was re-living this attitude in the telling and, when pressed on the point of his abiding faith in Chiang even after the utter collapse of the Nationalist government and army, Huang summed himself up as 'an extremely stubborn person and extremely reactionary'.

He was detained by the Military Justice department in the North China headquarters of the People's Liberation Army in Hebei province. He was alone here for some time before being removed to Peking, and it was during this period that, according to Cai Xingsan, Huang began reading the books on physics and mathematics that kindled an interest in mechanical invention. In Peking he was first accommodated in the so-called 'model' prison, a legacy from pre-Liberation days, from which Du Yuming and Song Xilian were released in December 1959. Huang, instead of gaining his freedom at the same time, was transferred then to a newly built prison on the outskirts of the city. This building, he said, resembled quarters for high-ranking cadres more than a place of detention for wrong-doers. It was well fitted out with library, recreation facilities and hospital. About 1967 he moved to Fushun, the Peking jail being needed for an influx of prisoners generated by the Cultural Revolution.

As soon as he entered his first regular prison, Huang was expected to begin the study of Marxism and Mao Zedong Thought. Attitudinally he was not ready for this, however: his fighting spirit was still to the fore. Good living conditions and a generous policy towards captives were not enough to overcome his resistance in those early years. It was not easy for him to change his thoughts, he said.

We asked him if he could identify the most potent influences on his attitudes and thoughts throughout the time of his imprisonment. His reply gave no emphasis to the organized study and criticism routines of the prisons. Certainly he described them for us, but they did not loom large in his recollections. This may be partly accounted for by his having spent a lot of his time on a sick bed, as we shall see; but it was clear nevertheless that he was more likely to be touched by good deeds and kindly attitudes than by more overt attempts at thought reform. 'My change took a long time and came by a roundabout way', he said. Huang singled out for special mention three significant inducements that led him to a favourable attitude towards the new China. These were the treatment he received during his serious illnesses, the conducted tours arranged for prisoners and the manner in which his family was accepted into the life of the new society.

It became apparent after his imprisonment that Huang was not well, and in 1952 he was diagnosed as suffering a severe infection of tuberculosis. He spent the next four years in bed under the best medical supervision. On top of rations permitted to patients in general, he was allowed a special diet which persisted until 1958 in its entirety and in some detail right up to 1967. He completely recovered from tuberculosis whereas he doubted if he could have survived at all had he been at large. Not only did he suffer tuberculosis, he also developed heart trouble in the late sixties and spent a good deal of his early Fushun time in that prison's infirmary. Again, a month before his release he had had a severe heart attack. Specialists were called from Shenyang and he was admitted to the first affiliated hospital of the Shenyang Medical School, a good modern institution. In fact it was while recovering here that he heard the order of pardon. The doctor in charge escorted him not only back to Fushun but also on to Peking for the reception by Ye Jianying, Vice-Chairman of the Chinese People's Political Consultative Conference. (This reception, incidentally, must have marked a full turn of the wheel for Huang. In 1923 Ye Jianying had been an instructor at the Whampoa Academy and had subsequently commanded a division in the Northern Expedition.)

The prison authorities arranged many visits and tours. These began in 1956 by which time Huang was over the worst of his tuberculosis. Some tours were long, some short, and they covered industry, agriculture and education and made contact with all levels of society. The contrast they revealed with the old China impressed Huang. He had taken the former situation for granted, but now began to see what could be accomplished through a changed political outlook. He spoke especially of the class education museums set up in many cities to bring home by means of models and displays the fact of the exploitation of one class by another.

Because he himself had come from a family living from rent, he had believed that it was part of the natural order that, by virtue of landlords, peasants were able to make a living rather than the converse. What is sadder, he is now prepared to concede, is that the peasants themselves had tended to believe this. Huang says that with these tours he came, though slowly, to recognize that he had, by his acquiescence, helped the continuation of such a society. Every May Day and National Day in Peking, prisoners were invited to watch the celebrations in the Tiananmen Square from the Public Security office on the top floor. Huang could observe on these occasions what appeared to be an improvement in the spirit of the people, but he was slow to see how this related to him — a war prisoner.

The treatment his family of wife, two sons and two daughters
received moved him very much, Huang said. In no other historical
period at a change of dynasty (as he put it) could he have expected to
live or have his family fare so well. After some early indecision, his
wife Cai Ruoshu and the children had resided on the mainland
throughout the period of Huang's imprisonment. Following her
husband's defeat and being uncertain whether he was still alive, she had
accepted an offer from the deputy commander of the Nationalist
Air Force to be flown to Taiwan with his family. With three young
children as well as a new baby born during the Huai-Hai campaign, it
could not have been easy for Huang's wife to decide on the best plan.
She was not long in Taiwan when, uneasy at having distanced herself
from her husband, she returned alone and visited Shanghai where she
learnt on good authority that her husband was alive but in captivity.
This was enough to persuade her. She went back to Taiwan, collected
her children and then returned to settle in Shanghai. That was in 1950.
She obtained a position in the Shanghai City Library and worked there
until her retirement in 1963. The children all received a good education
with government assistance. One son graduated from Zhejiang
University having majored in engineering and is now the head of a
technical division in a factory in Jiangxi province. The second son
graduated from university in Nanjing, having studied agricultural
science. He made some serious mistakes at times (Huang laughed as he
mentioned this), but he is now back teaching at Shandong University.
The older daughter, Minnan, herself now married with two children,
teaches physics at Peking's Qinghua University. She graduated from
Fudan University in Shanghai in 1956. The younger daughter, Huinan,
was in the last class but one of high school when the Cultural
Revolution began in 1966. She participated in some of the revolutionary
activities of the period — burning of old photographs and other
traditional objects at home, travelling with her group to Peking and
Wuhan — and without further study was deemed in 1967 to have
graduated from high school. She went down to the countryside in
1969 and was there for six years until her father's release, upon which
she was recalled and given a position in the Ministry of Health in
Peking. Originally appointed as a worker in the pharmaceuticals
examination office, she is now a technician cadre and is also enrolled
as a student with the TV University. She did not meet her father until
1975, but Huang had visits from his wife and elder daughter as early as
1956. There was unmistakable gratitude in the old man's voice as he
talked about the family. Whatever may have been his ideological

stance as a result of efforts made to reform him during his long confinement, there could be little doubt that the regard shown by authorities for his wife and children had predisposed him to think approvingly of them.

Although Huang was prepared to admit he had been emotionally touched by the Communists' solicitude for his health and for the welfare of his family, and although he was genuinely impressed by some of the tangible evidence of improvements in the nation at large, intellectually he stood aloof. Withstanding repeated criticism and haranguing from co-prisoners as well as the assiduous efforts of prison tutors, he would not address himself to the study of political theory. It is my impression that he maintains that position still in spite of his membership of the Standing Committee of the fifth National Committee of the People's Political Consultative Conference. When tackled in prison for not attending to his proper duty as a political prisoner and not devoting himself to the study of the set documents, he refused to admit that his dedication to scientific enquiry was an escape from re-education. On the contrary, he insisted that what he was attempting was much more profitable to China than admitting past crimes and reading articles like Chairman Mao's 'On Protracted War' (*SW*, II: 113-94). 'I get fed up reading about war', one of his co-prisoners recollected him as exclaiming, 'I made mistakes in battle and I don't want anything more to do with fighting, I only want to do scientific research. My dedication to scientific research represents a change in my life: therein lies my re-education' (Cai, August 1979).

In the 1950s, not only had the other prisoners been mobilized to bear pressure on Huang, but the prison authorities had also called on his wife and on ·Academy scientists to persuade him that his ideas for a self-perpetuating machine were erroneously based and his energies misdirected. It was not until he came within Jin Yuan's ambit in Fushun that he found any sympathetic encouragement, and what he received then was encouragement in a very tangible form. Instead of trying to argue the would-be inventor out of what others had called a crazy scheme, he gave orders for the prison factory to make a model after Huang's specifications. Draughtsmen were engaged to draw up proper blueprints and a wooden scale model was constructed. It did not promise well but the work of producing an accurate prototype in metal went ahead. In materials alone the· cost must have run into thousands of yuan to say nothing of the wages of designers, metal workers and electricians. After a couple of months of activity, the machine was ready for testing and Jin Yuan, the prison cadres and those prisoners who had worked on the project assembled with its originator for the grand test. There was a good deal of excitement as Huang pressed the button to activate the machine electrically followed by anxious anticipation as the current was then switched off. The machine continued for a minute or two, slowed down and stopped. Anticlimax. Then Jin, in a move that showed his purpose to have run deeper than a mere humouring of an elderly crank, offered the disappointed Huang his continuing support and that of the government. 'This is only the first attempt', he said. 'Draw what lessons you can from the experiment and do some more research.' Others might have thought that the failure of the test would convince Huang of the futility of his efforts, but Jin had a keener appreciation of the qualities of the man with whom he was dealing. It is surely not too fanciful to attribute Huang Wei's submissive address at the reception following the final amnesty to Jin Yuan's masterly strategy. The lion had become a lamb.

In two long interview sessions Huang retraced his life and we repeatedly observed flashes of his former fiery temperament, but when, in a final question, we asked what he saw now as to be his chief contribution, he slid into the conventional rhetoric of the moment: he wished to help the restoration of Taiwan and to contribute to the four modernizations.

Perhaps this answer was not entirely empty of real promise. Were Huang to be granted entry into Taiwan, he might have as much influence with former colleagues and subordinates as anyone else from the mainland, and, with respect to the modernization of industry, the more recent development in his scientific thinking along the lines of a gravity machine may not be without practical merit.

6 PUJIE: ONCE A PRINCE

Aixinjueluo Pujie: so reads in *hanyu pinyin* the Manchu name of the brother of China's last emperor, Xuan Tong (Puyi). Born in 1907, he was the second son of Prince Chun and a year younger than Puyi who was made Emperor at the age of three in 1908. An examination of his family tree reveals him to be nephew of the Emperor Guang Xu (1875-1908) and grand-nephew on two counts of the Empress-Dowager, Cixi. Although his father was the Prince Regent, the family (apart from the boy Emperor himself) continued to live outside the Forbidden City. Their home was an imposing mansion, the Bei Fu, situated in the extreme north of Peking on the shores of the lake known as Shisha hai. In this way, Pujie was kept apart from some of the most debilitating influences of court life which his brother, brought up entirely within the precincts of the Forbidden City, breathed in daily. In fact, Pujie recalls, it was not until he was about ten years old that he met his imperial brother on his first visit to the palace. It should be noted that, under the terms of the 'Articles of Favourable Treatment' drawn up at the establishment of the Republic in 1911, life continued as before for the imperial family. Titles and ceremonies were preserved, and the subsidies allocated by the government were of such magnitude that the climate of licence and corruption that had long since evolved around the throne continued virtually undiminished to sustain and foment the Imperial Household Department (*Nei Wu Fu*) and its numerous attendant eunuchs.

Although Pujie did not dwell constantly in this atmosphere, he must certainly have been influenced by it. By the time he was 15 years old, his home tutorials were being supplemented by studies undertaken within the palace, and from then on there developed a close and lasting attachment between the two brothers. At the time of the Emperor's marriage in 1922, Pujie was made a Fuguo Gong — a duke of the second order — and the following year we find him implicated in an attempt to help his brother escape from the Forbidden City. Puyi was being held a virtual prisoner to serve the personal interests of officers of the Nei Wu Fu whose anachronistic court would otherwise collapse. For their ends alone was it that the young Emperor was forced to lead such an unnatural and sheltered existence. There are many evidences that the young man himself wanted to penetrate the fastnesses of tradition and come to terms with the modern world, and who better was there to turn to in this desire than his less circumscribed brother, Pujie? The attempt this time failed however. Indeed, Puyi did not become a free agent until many years had passed. Some would argue that even in his last years he remained trapped in a lifestyle dictated wholly by others. This question of freedom of mind is one that has to be addressed in the case of each of the principal subjects of this enquiry. Meanwhile, a quick outline of Puyi's career will help set Pujie in context.

Puyi wrenched himself free of the Nei Wu Fu eventually in 1924 only to become the political plaything of the Japanese who guaranteed him safety in their concession in Tianjin. This seven-year protection paid off for the Japanese when they came to set up the Manchu kingdom in China's north-east. Puyi then found himself brought out of storage and appointed as 'Chief Executive' and later, in 1934, as Emperor — but a puppet emperor, responsive only to the strings of Japanese military power. After the defeat of the Japanese in 1945, came five years in the Soviet Union as prisoner of the Russians, and then followed a further ten years of imprisonment back in China after the Communist victory in 1949.

Pujie was at hand throughout much of his brother's unfortunate life until its end through cancer in 1967; but, at least up until 1945, being of less importance politically, he was able to experience life more broadly.

What follows is what Pujie chose to tell us briefly about his life in interview. His first regular schooling began in 1929 when he was in his early twenties. This was at the Tokyo College of Studies where he studied Japanese, English and German. During this period the Japanese military authorities engaged him in unofficial talks that presaged the invasion of Manchuria and the possible role there might be for his brother to play. He returned briefly to China and then, after the 'Mukden Incident' of 1931, undertook military training in Japan and became a platoon commander in a Japanese infantry unit in Changchun. He later went back again for officer training at Japan's top military academy in preparation for high office in the Military Affairs Department of the new Manchu 'kingdom'. During this period, too, the Japanese authorities arranged a marriage for Pujie with Saga Hiro, daughter of a noble Japanese family. The wedding took place in 1937.

It seems clear from Pujie's recital so far that he was being consciously and deliberately groomed for an important role in the regime of which his brother was nominally head. How free he might have been to reject this role may only be guessed at. Pujie is a lineal descendant of Nurhaci who founded the Manchu dynasty in 1616, and the vision of his ancient family returning for ever to its ancestral home was probably so commanding that, willingly or unwillingly, he became entangled in a clever Japanese ruse. Whatever was the extent of his real freedom, Pujie is today ready to confess that he has to accept some of the responsibility for the part he played. He told Cai Xingsan in 1979:

> Puyi and I had always dreamed of building the empire of Aixinjueluo. We treated China as the private property of our family. It has been very stupid of us to try to do something against the trend of history. We tried to stop the wheel from moving forward and, as a result, we were almost crushed to death by it.
>
> (Cai, June 1979)

To resume Pujie's story: he and his brother, attempting a flight to Japan when the Japanese were defeated in 1945, fell into Russian hands and were taken off to the Soviet Union for five years. They were returned to China in 1950 at the request of the newly established Communist government and the two awaited their reception in trepidation. They could not suppose any less punishment than execution, considering what they had gathered about the Reds' reputation for ruthlessness. In the face of this expectation, the fact that they were courteously received disconcerted them. An entire PLA company met them when their train arrived at the border and Pujie was startled to notice that the company's commander was one of his own former cadets. He thought better of approaching him but, when the commander made the first move, they fell to reminiscing about former times and old friendships. Pujie broached the question of his own future and this gave the commander the opportunity to expound Chairman Mao's policy of re-education for former enemies of the people.

At Shenyang (formerly Mukden), a reception was staged for the former emperor by the commander-in-chief of the district. In fact, so elaborate was the occasion that Puyi appeared not to know how to interpret what was happening. Was this a ritual preparation for their execution or an indication that they could expect a very early release?

The answer was to be neither. They were put into prison, there to stay until they were re-educated. This turned out to be nine years for one brother and ten for the other.

But the Fushun prison was not a bad place in which to be. Pujie spoke of the skilled medical treatment they received and the special food rations. The prisoners were encouraged to enjoy themselves. They could play mahjong – provided they made the set themselves. They gambled with the extra cigarettes issued at New Year. They were encouraged to stage their own Peking opera, for which equipment was provided. Pujie did some script-writing for stage plays and occasionally acted in them. The prison also had a good lending library. All in all, their entertainment, recreation and general living standards were well attended to and an atmosphere of enjoyment was actively fostered.

The Fushun prison and the centre where they had been detained in the Soviet Union differed markedly in style. The Russians had compelled them to do menial work: in China they were encouraged rather than compelled. Russian guards had carried pistols: the Chinese did not. Even when some prisoners might be cutting cabbages in the vegetable plots the guards remained unarmed though the prisoners themselves were using knives. Pujie was also impressed by the contrast between the treatment they were receiving in Fushun and what he knew had happened to prisoners under the Japanese occupation.

Of course, the prisoners were expected to reform themselves: this was why they were there. But even the reform programme did not appear to be forced. It seemed to Pujie that their essays in self criticism (*jiantao*) were written of their own free will.

After a few months at Fushun, Pujie had a letter from his family living in Japan. When, in 1945, plans were being made for Puyi and Pujie to flee to Japan it was decided that the womenfolk would proceed separately. After an eventful 16 months, Pujie's wife, Hiro, accompanied by their younger daughter, Husheng, rejoined Huisheng, the older daughter, and other members of the family, in their native Japan. Apart from knowing that her husband had fallen into Russian hands, she had quite lost touch with him. The next she learnt of him was from a newspaper report in 1950 that he had been returned to China, but still there was no direct communication. The initiative was taken by Huisheng, now a twelve-year-old high school girl. She wrote to the Chinese premier, Zhou Enlai, not telling her mother. In her letter she asked the whereabouts of her father and permission to write to him, and a reply came back from the State Council giving the address and the requested permission. Pujie knew nothing of these circumstances until after his release years later, but he was delighted to receive a letter from his wife and they communicated regularly thereafter.

This anecdote is not the only one that could be related to exemplify the interest shown by state leaders. Chairman Mao himself came into the picture a year or so before Pujie was released. The Chairman told Zai Tao, brother of Prince Chun, that his two nephews were progressing very well with their reform in prison and that he might do well to visit them there and learn from them. Zai did subsequently visit the prison and actually spent a few days with Puyi and Pujie without supervision. We were not told whether Uncle Zai went away any happier with the new society, or better informed, but his two nephews were much encouraged by the visit.

They also received visits from time to time from key Communist officials. At first, Pujie declared, this made them feel like animals in a zoo; but gradually they came to welcome these visitors because of their kind and considerate manner. Among them were He Long and Nie Rongzhen, both members of the Central Committee of the Chinese Communist Party.

Pujie's release from prison in 1960 (one year after his brother's release) was marked by considerable assistance in rehabilitation. With Zhou Enlai's encouragement, though against Puyi's advice, his wife came back to join him in China. His second daughter also accompanied her mother but later returned to Japan where she now lives with her husband and four children. (The first daughter had died in 1957.) Pujie and Hiro set up a ménage that included Puyi in a large courtyard-style house situated at no. 52 Huguosi and at no great distance from the Forbidden City. It was not the Bei Fu mentioned earlier, but it had also been owned by his father and was now renovated under government authorization, furnished, and supplied with a maid. The reunited couple were given special permits to purchase household goods at the lowest prices and Pujie was granted an annual government allowance which, together with a legacy of ¥10,000 from his father (who had died in 1951), means that he lives comfortably. He described his sixteen-room house as 'better than average', a description equally apt for his well-cut suit, his stylish boots, elegant cigarette case, and general appearance as we saw him.

Cai Xingsan, who visited Pujie's home recently, wrote of it as looking quite imposing from the outside with two tall gates painted black. The gate handles are of metal engraved with a tiger's head. Positioned on either side is a pair of sculptured guards. The house boasts a beautifully landscaped central garden with chrysanthemums, bonsai and flowering trees. A large reception room is divided in two by a Chinese screen so that two groups of visitors may be received at the one time. Rosewood coffee tables and chairs are arranged on both sides and the whole is fully carpeted and decorated with potted plants and vases of flowers. Chandeliers hang from the ceiling. The appearance, wrote Cai, is elegant and luxurious (Cai, May 1979).

It is clear that Pujie, now in the eighth decade of his life, leads a comfortable life. He even weathered the Cultural Revolution with little discomfort. But what do we know of his re-education? In our interviews in Peking, Pujie had little to say about his own thoughts, attitudes and beliefs or about the processes by which he arrived at them. We sought some opinion on this question in Fushun. There, one of the prison officers, Sun Shiqiang, made a few comments. Pujie, he said, shared some of the views of his brother, the emperor, when they first came to Fushun. He doubted, for example, the sincerity of the Communists, but under considerable and consistent treatment re-education gradually occurred. It had proceeded far enough by July 1956 for Pujie to be called upon to give evidence for the prosecution at the trial in Shenyang of some former Japanese administrators in the puppet regime of which they had been part.

Of the two brothers, Pujie appeared the more able. According to Sun, much of Puyi's autobiography (Aisin-Gioro Pu Yi, 1964-5) was written by Pujie, and in manual labour, too, he was the more capable though the demands placed on them were not great — just enough, Sun said, to let them know the meaning of work. Pujie did some translating of Japanese literature into Chinese.

By and large, according to Sun, Pujie participated actively through-out his imprisonment, and he was not noticeably any more difficult than his brother in the matter of reform. One wonders, then, why he should have been kept a year longer. One of the other prison officers, Wang Daojian, thought that he was more difficult to reform than Puyi, and he attributed this to the impediments of a Japanese training and a higher level of education. Had Pujie, then, fulfilled the requirements for release in 1960? The prison officers claimed so, but there is on record a snatch of conversation from the reception given by Zhou Enlai in 1961 when Hiro arrived from Japan and the family was re-united. At mention of his elder daughter's tragic death a few years before, Zhou said to Hiro, 'I am sorry for your loss', and turning then to Puyi and Pujie he told them, 'Don't forget, that was why you were let out so early!' (McAleavy, 1963: 278).

7 ZHANG JINGZHU: WILLING SOLDIER, RELUCTANT STUDENT

Ex-prisoner Zhang Jingzhu, having been acquainted with the late Hu Yunhong, claimed continuing friendship with the Hu family, and, through correspondence with his relatives, J.P. learnt that 'uncle' Zhang would be happy to talk to him about his father. Accordingly we set off for Chengdu to meet him, but we made no advance arrangements and no point of explaining our mission to the authorities there. These omissions were not without consequence. During the 30 hours following our arrival in Chengdu, we became painfully aware of the existence of a maze-like network that many visitors to China, moving under skilful guidance, seldom perceive or even suspect. Renounce the offices of a guide however and paths that begin with promise may lead to dead ends: one can imagine having stumbled into a Kafka script of unreason.

Approached to help us find Zhang Jingzhu, an official of the Chengdu branch of the China Travel Service seemed co-operative enough and led us to expect a telephone call at our hotel by 10.00 a.m. to the effect that a meeting had been arranged. When the call had not come by the appointed time, J.P. rang to say that unless he was to hear by 11.00 he would engage a car and attempt to find Zhang without official help. Just before 11.00 the Travel Service telephoned to say that a car had been arranged to go to Zhang's address but that there could be no guarantee that anyone would be found at home. J.P. accepted the opportunity this offer presented, only to return to the hotel at 12.45 p.m. without having yet seen his 'uncle'. Neighbours in the same courtyard at Zhang's address had said that he had gone to a study session at the western branch of the People's Political Consultative Conference, whereupon J.P. had hied off there only to learn that Zhang had already left for home. J.P. then retraced his path and waited at the home well beyond the time that neighbours said the usually punctual Zhang would regularly have returned. Thus it became clear that, if we were going to meet 'uncle' Zhang at all, it would not be purely on our terms.

We did meet Zhang — on two occasions. At 3.15 that same afternoon he arrived unaccompanied at our hotel room. During the ensuing exchange of courtesies it was established that his acquaintance with Hu senior had begun in the Fushun prison where they had both been

41

inmates from 1956 to 1975. We began therefore to question him about his long imprisonment and the events leading up to it. The conversation did not get very far before Zhang explained that he had intended this visit as a social call only and that he would now like to arrange a further meeting to comply with our wishes but he had to inform his branch of the Political Consultative Conference. He made some apology for the difficulties we had encountered in the morning and said he looked forward to seeing us again the following afternoon. It was then 3.45 p.m.

The following day at 2.10 p.m. Zhang returned, still alone, ready to tell his story. In the interim, J.P. had explained to our contact in the Travel Service the nature of our purpose. Part of the way through the ensuing discussion, which appeared now to be uninhibited, Zhang left briefly to return with a friend, 'uncle' Chen, an elderly man of his own age, who had served under Hu Yunhong in the days when the latter had been a county administrator in Jiangxi province. He, however, took little part in the conversation that followed. Zhang's account did not add much to the accounts already obtained in Peking and Fushun, but it has value to the extent to which it corroborates these others and in that it was related in different circumstances. It is worth recording that at no time was a cadre present during these discussions.

Zhang was born in Hubei province in 1906, but he spent his early career as a soldier in neighbouring Sichuan and it was to Sichuan that he returned after his release from prison in 1975. Sichuan, separated geographically from the rest of China by high mountains, was, in the 1920s and early 1930s, also largely aloof from the nation's political concerns. It had its own. Several old-style warlords vied for influence and each commanded armed troops. One of the more prominent of these was 'Marshall' Liu Xiang. Liu continued throughout his life to be an important figure in Sichuan. For some years he was effective governor of the province, continuing in that role beyond the arrival of the Chiang Kai-shek government in Chongqing in 1937 and up to his death the following year. Zhang joined his army in 1927. By 1935 he had his own command of about 150 men.

In May of that year, the concerns of the rest of China were brought forcibly to the attention of the Sichuanese. Communist troops of the First Front Army under Zhu De (himself a native of Sichuan) crossed the Yangtze into Sichuan from Yunnan. Sichuanese troops opposed these 'bandits' passing through their territory, but the Communists advanced nevertheless. Their crossing of the Dadu river remains one of the imagination-firing episodes of the Long March. The following month saw the rendezvous in west Sichuan between the First Army and the Fourth Front Army led by Zhang Guotao and the resulting discussions about the future course of the Long March. These were events of tremendous significance in the history of the Communist revolution and, in view of Zhang Jingzhu's later engagements with and fate at the hands of the Red Army, it is interesting that he should have been so close to them.

The next date to emerge from Zhang's story was 1943. The Nationalist headquarters had retreated under Japanese threat five years before to Chongqing, and, holed up there in the mists of Sichuan, Chiang Kai-shek had just finished putting into writing his analysis of and solution for the predicament that China now darkly found herself in. As a practical measure along with the publication of *China's Destiny*, Chiang was consolidating his armed forces including the incorporation of a number of hitherto independent armed units. Zhang was one officer who joined the regular Nationalist army, but not without an initial setback. As a Lieutenant-Colonel and Deputy Regimental Commander in the late Liu Xiang's unit, Zhang Jingzhu pictured himself immediately occupying an important post in the Nationalist force. But a commission without formal training was unthinkable to Chiang Kai-shek for whom form always rated highly. Zhang undertook a four-week course at the Central Military Academy in Sichuan, a token that made him acceptable for a senior appointment. He had a post in Anhui province in 1945, and in 1947 was detailed briefly to Taiwan to assist in suppressing an anti-Chiang uprising there. By October 1947 he was promoted to command a regiment in Jiangsu province with the rank of colonel, and so came into a position where he all but shared with hundreds of thousands of men and their officers a shattering defeat by Communist forces at the battle of the Huai-Hai a little more than a year later. This was the battle in which Generals Du Yuming and Huang Wei lost their freedom. In fact, Zhang was able to withdraw with his men to south of the Yangtze where he hoped to participate in a bid to protect Shanghai from invasion. The bid was in vain however. The Liberation Army also crossed the great river. Peace terms proposed by the now clearly victorious Communists on 15 April were rejected by the Nanking government on 20 April (*SW* IV: 390-6) and Zhang was injured in action and captured on the very next day, 21 April 1949.

On capture, Zhang underwent an emergency operation in an army field hospital and then, while convalescing, was sent to Suzhou for re-education in the 'tenth training regiment for liberated officers'. Here he attended study sessions based mainly on the writings of Mao Zedong, in particular 'On New Democracy' (*SW*, II: 339-84) and 'On Coalition Government' (*SW*, III: 205-70), essays that analyzed the revolution and set out a blueprint for China and a new Chinese culture. His understanding was that this re-education period would be fairly short and that all captured soldiers who were prepared to make some acknowledgement of their error would soon be free to go their own way. It seems however that, following the formal establishment of the People's Republic later in the year, the policy of the Communist Party towards reform became stricter. Even so, he hardly expected that he would spend the next 26 years of his life in prison.

After his recovery from his injury, he had spells of imprisonment in Shanghai, in Shandong province, in Nanjing and finally in Fushun, where he was admitted in 1956.

Zhang spoke of the prison routines. There appears to have been more emphasis in the first prisons he experienced than at Fushun on the labour aspect of reform. The days were spent half in study and half in labour, the latter consisting usually of vegetable raising, pig rearing and the like. In these activities, the staff were as hard-working as the prisoners. On the study side, criticism sessions were an important part of the programme: if either labour or study were not being done properly one was likely to incite the criticism of one's fellow prisoners. Seldom did staff members intervene in these sessions and then only to ensure that they were being conducted properly.

A feature of the early years in Fushun were tours conducted to educate prisoners at first hand about the achievements of the new China. Zhang personally found these trips to nearby Shenyang and other places very helpful. Factories, steel mills, and museums designed to raise the level of class consciousness were included. These tours, the recreational activities and the attitude of the prison staff combined to produce a fairly encouraging atmosphere in the Fushun prison. He was all the more disappointed, therefore, when he found that he was not to be released on the occasion of the amnesty for war criminals announced in September 1959. He would, he then realised, have to make a greater effort in the matter of his own reform.

When asked if he knew why his release was so long delayed, Zhang admitted that, before 1959, he was rather confused and hesitant in the face of the expectations placed before him. Having been a Regimental Commander, he was being expected to recall all the actions, not only his own, but also those of his officers and men. This was unrealistic of his captors, he thought, and anxiety over meeting these demands combined with a growing anxiety for the welfare of his family to take toll of him physically during these early prison years. He became very thin and, especially during the years 1953 to 1957, suffered a lot from stomach bleeding.

After that first disappointing 1959 amnesty, several more followed — in September 1959, November 1960, December 1961, March 1963. Still Zhang was not released. Then came the Cultural Revolution and for a while the Fushun prison became a less inviting place. The prison was taken over by the People's Liberation Army from Public Security, the staff (including Jin Yuan) were sent away for retraining, and prisoners were no longer encouraged to write or take part in plays and other recreational activities as before. Film showings were reduced from two to one a week. Communication with the outside world and with families became more difficult.

The years dragged on and hope of release faded. Indeed the seeming hopelessness of his situation led his wife to seek a divorce. Although this made him even more miserable, he could see that for her it was probably best and he wrote a letter agreeing to the separation. There is, however, a bright element in this story. The letter of course had to pass through the prison authorities before being sent off and, after reading it, a sympathetic officer called Zhang up for a chat, seeking to establish whether he still had an emotional attachment to his wife. Zhang admitted that he had but that to release her was the kindest thing he could do in the circumstances. He was not to discover the outcome of this discussion until he was set free in 1975. He found then that action on the part of the Fushun prison authorities had successfully blocked the divorce and that furthermore his wife was still willing to receive him back and to assist in his rehabilitation.

Zhang Jingzhu was plainly wearied by the long years in prison, but, even so, he felt bound to speak well of the treatment received at the hands of the Fushun cadres. Their great merit lay in an ability to interpret policy and to realize it. They preached and practised, he said, the ideal of 'a sound mind in a sound body'.

8   CAI XINGSAN: YOUNGEST GENERAL

Cai Xingsan, now living in Hong Kong, has the air of a successful businessman and gives no hint in his appearance that he spent what should have been the best years of his life as a prisoner in his native China. From the age of 32 to the age of 56 he was locked away for being on the wrong side of the political fence. Our interview with him in Hong Kong came less than four years after his release from prison and one might have predicted some traces of bitterness to emerge during a three or four hour conversation. This prediction unfulfilled, we asked him about it over dinner following the interview. 'I could not feel bitter against people who not only refrained from physically maltreating me but who also always regarded me as a person', was his response. Nevertheless, he went on to point out, the 'spiritual' pressure had been considerable and this had been hard to take.

Cai was born in 1919 in Jiangxi province. Not much about his early years came out in interview, but we do know that, in the years immediately after the Japanese surrender of 1945, he was in Shanghai writing articles on the economy. Shanghai, along with Nanjing, was at the economic, industrial and political heart of Chiang's regime, and it was to Shanghai as head of that city's Economic Supervisory Office that Chiang appointed his 39-year old son, Jiang Jingguo, on the latter's return from Russia. Jiang Jingguo's task was to try to bring about economic stability to the city, crippled by runaway inflation. He set about implementing the new currency edict of August 1948 with a ruthlessness that could have brought no joy to anyone but the Four Great Families who stood to gain all from the government-run monopolies. It is not certain how much Cai Xingsan's analysis of Shanghai's economy influenced Jiang's policy, but the two established a friendship. When, subsequent to the occupation of Shanghai by the Communists in the following May, Jiang was detailed by the Guomindang to organize the Jiangxi province Nationalist Youth Corps, he called on Cai to lead it and, although his friend had had no previous military experience, accorded him the rank of general. Cai was only 30 years old. The express purpose of the Youth Corps was to suppress Communist activity, and to assist in this it was as fully equipped as any regular army unit. This, however, was not enough to ensure its success.

While Cai and his corps were preparing to move into the mountain regions near the province's eastern border with Fujian, they were engaged by troops from the People's Liberation Army. Cai was among those caught. This was his first contact with the PLA and he recalls how impressed he was to find that, far from being unruly bandits, they observed all the conventions and treated him according to his rank. They allowed him the use of a horse and the company of four of his aides. The Red Army was on the move, however, and supervision was not tight. Cai took advantage of this laxity to make an escape.

Once free, he made for his native place, Shangrao, in the northeast of the province, hoping to find supporters there and the opportunity to reorganize his troops. He found friends who gave him protection and permitted him to hide, but he received no assistance in reforming his unit.

He managed to keep a low profile until, with the outbreak of the Korean war in 1950 and the accompanying mounting concern with internal security, a campaign was launched for the suppression of counter-revolutionaries. He was tracked down and brought for interview before the district head and section chief of the provincial arm of Public Security. He was treated courteously and asked for his political views. He explained his anti-Communist stance saying that he looked upon the Communists as mere stooges or running dogs of the Russians. If China were to go all the way with the Russians, he said, it would be worse than being lost to the United States under Guomindang rule. The substance of his interviewers' response was that he lacked any evidence or insight into the policy of the Communist Party and how it intended to govern and, accordingly, his fears were unfounded. He really ought to make a closer study. He was not further detained after the interview and he remembers that shortly afterwards he did attempt to evaluate the changed situation by analysing the new government's economic measures and relating them to Mao's speeches and theories. In fact he wrote a paper on the question for submission to the authorities.

It may be thought that Cai was now about to enter into an agreeable relationship with Communism; but, as he put it, although the authorities were lenient, the masses were not. After all, the central targets of the current campaign were members of those Nationalist bodies, such as the Youth Corps, that had been especially committed to the elimination of Communist elements. What guarantee did the ordinary people have that Cai would not again attempt to sabotage the revolution? In April 1951 he was called up again. This time it was not for a gentlemanly discussion but for trial at a mass meeting to be confronted with the most serious charge of counter-revolutionary activity. He was one of many. Forty were sentenced at this particular trial, of whom six were executed. He himself was given the death sentence but with a stay of two years and the opportunity to show whether this should be commuted to imprisonment accompanied by reform through labour. The commutation came to pass and he began his reform in a factory attached to the Nanchang prison, making buttons from mother-of-pearl. Turning the situation to advantage (something Cai always attempted), he was soon writing a paper on the technique of producing goods from mother-of-pearl and finding himself promoted from factory hand to the position of technician.

In 1956, Cai was one of ten prisoners from the Nanchang area sent to Wuhan, whither all the war criminals from the southern and central regions of China were assembled in the second half of that year. From Wuhan, the prisoners were redistributed. Some were sent to Shandong province, some to Shanxi province, the largest number going to Fushun in Liaoning province. Fushun received prisoners mainly of high and middle rank and Cai was one of these.

Cai agrees that Fushun was probably the best prison camp in China. Although there were watchtowers, guards were not in evidence. Since leaving prison in 1975, Cai has published articles in Hong Kong relating his experiences and showing the Fushun prison in a good light. Just as at Nanchang, so also at Fushun, Cai took the initiative to improve his lot. He set about organizing a committee on learning to arrange series of lectures given both by inmates and by people invited from outside. He was able to have these lectures incorporated within regular study sessions known as 'collective self-education'. Cai's committee continued up to the onset of the Cultural Revolution when it was disbanded, control of the prison passing for the time being from Public Security to the army.

In an attempt to assess why Cai had to wait until the 1975 amnesty for his release from prison, we questioned him on any difficulty he might have had in confessing his crimes during his re-education. He declared that the main difficulty arose from his anti-Soviet stance. He was prepared, he said, to accept Communism as an alternative solution for the world, but he could find nothing admirable in Stalin's Russia. When in time the split came between China and the Soviet Union, he felt vindicated in the stand he had taken. In this statement there is no sufficient explanation for long-term rather than short-term imprisonment and the question must be returned to in a later chapter.

Cai was one of the ten who, on release at the time of the 1975 amnesty, accepted the Chinese government's offer of assistance to transfer to Taiwan. In the event, the Taiwanese authorities would not accept him. Cai believes that, in so refusing, the Taiwan government showed an almost unbelievable degree of political ineptitude. This did much to shape Cai's favourable attitude towards the People's Republic, an attitude he clearly has, even if he prefers to express it from the commercially more opportune Hong Kong.

9 DUAN KEWEN: SCEPTIC

> You may object that it is not a trial at all.
>
> (Franz Kafka, *The Trial*)

We had sought the interview with Hong Kong resident, Cai Xingsan, hoping to check some of the bias we knew would inevitably influence the accounts of imprisonment and reform obtained within the People's Republic itself. We found his account not markedly different in either descriptive detail or tone from others already gathered. It seemed important to look further.

Of the ten men among the 293 released in the final 1975 amnesty who elected to leave the mainland in the vain hope of settling in Taiwan, at least two went to the United States. One of these, Duan Kewen, had begun writing some memoirs in the form of newspaper articles in 1976 and Amnesty International had drawn on these, presenting some of his prison experiences in an unfavourable light.

At the time of our visit to China our only information about Duan had come from the Amnesty International report and we raised with our hosts in Peking the allegation that Duan had been fettered and inhumanely treated. They did not reject the story. Nie Zhen, while claiming that Party policy on the treatment of prisoners was clear, consistent and humane, admitted the possibility of abnormalities of practice in some places. Not everyone had understood Party policy as they ought to have. After all, Nie pointed out, the People's Republic in its early days, in prison as in all walks of life, had had to rely on officials many of whom had no background or experience of Party policy. Certainly, however, the alleged maltreatment had not occurred while Duan had been in the Fushun prison, although it had to be conceded that even there he had been a difficult and obstinate character.

It seemed likely that Duan's account, even of Fushun, might be far less sympathetic than any already obtained, so it was important to examine and assess what he had written.

Duan was first detained in 1951 and, after being in several centres and prisons, spent eighteen and a half years to 1975 in the Fushun prison. He recounted his experiences in the New York Chinese language newspaper *Shijie Ribao* (*World Journal*) as a series of articles 28 of which were later re-published in Taiwan in book form. (Duan, 1978 and

50

1980) It is this re-published collection that is the source of our information about Duan. The articles do not appear to have been originally
intended for publication in book form: they are disconnected and
repetitive and some of the titles, like sub-editors' headings, promise
something different from what follows. Nevertheless they are rich in
description and anecdote and, importantly from our point of view, they
are far from dispassionate: Duan was ever ready to attribute ulterior
motives to the officials under whose surveillance he found himself.

In so far as Duan speaks of the reasons for his initial detention and
subsequent sentence to long-term imprisonment, he does so in his
articles defensively. If he was reluctant to admit his 'crimes' to the
police and prison officials then, he was not going to say much about
them now that any necessity had passed. Some inferences as to why
he became a marked man can nevertheless be drawn from the account
he has written of his life.

He was born in 1908 in Jilin province and received an education to
university level. He interrupted his secondary schooling for a while to
serve in a guerrilla unit and afterwards, in 1934, he joined a political
cadres' class in the Central Military Academy. On graduation from
there and during the early forties he moved about extensively and as
far afield as Yunnan and Sichuan, sometimes in the army (which he
says he did not enjoy) and sometimes in business. It was while he was
in Chongqing in 1945 that he accepted a commission under Dai Li in
the Guomindang's secret service organization, the Bureau of
Investigation and Statistics of the Military Council. Although he was
accorded the rank of Major-General, he claims to have been reluctant
to join the organization let alone carry out the tasks that were to be
allotted to him.

One sensitive mission he found especially distasteful. Because he
had been a classmate of Zhang Xuesi, he was chosen to try to persuade
him to defect. Zhang Xuesi was the son of the late Zhang Zuolin, one-
time military dictator of Manchuria, and the younger brother of Zhang
Xueliang whose kidnapping of Chiang Kai-shek at Xi'an in 1936 had
forced the latter's agreement to a united Nationalist-Communist front
against the Japanese invaders. The young Zhang had been on the side
of the Communists since early in the Sino-Japanese war and, now that
that war was concluded, he was nominated by them as Chairman of
the Liaoning provincial government in anticipation of the eventual
Communist take-over in the north-east. It was precisely this take-over
that the Nationalists were desperate to prevent and the defection of a
key person like Zhang would assist in a very complex and difficult

situation. If Duan's statement is correct, he must have let his side down badly in this matter. He claims to have soft-pedalled deliberately and to have done little about the matter.

About this time too, Duan commanded a task force in Liaoning province charged with supervising the restoration of administration and property to the central Nationalist government following the Japanese surrender. The Russian forces in the north-east had agreed to hand over only to representatives of the Nationalist government and not to the Communists. Duan does not tell how well he succeeded in this assignment, but it must have brought him into direct confrontation with the Communists.

There is a sense of relief in Duan's writing as he goes on to record Dai Li's accidental death in 1946 and of how he grasped this opportunity to leave the secret service organization. The reader is left wondering about the real nature of the hold that Dai had over Duan Kewen. On leaving the organization, he accepted an offer from the Nationalist governor of Jilin province to become a government adviser in Changchun, the capital. He records that during this period he once acted as a county administrator for a period of eight days, a seemingly minor detail that was to appear prominently in his later confessions. He was an eye-witness to the siege of Changchun and when the Communists succeeded in taking over in October 1948, he fled to Peking where he endeavoured to lie low under an assumed name, first as a small stall-holder and later as a dealer in paintings and scrolls.

When during the 1950-1 campaign for the suppression of counter-revolutionaries the authorities called on citizens to come forward and disclose their past errors, Duan made a declaration about his brief spell as a county administrator. He said nothing about his connection with the Guomindang secret service organization. From then on he came increasingly under observation until his arrest on 2 February 1951. The Peking police sent him to Changchun where, along with about 20 others, he was required to write his autobiography. Still he withheld his connection with the secret service, was accused of covering up his past and was not only locked up in the Changchun prison but put into leg irons as well. He claims to have remained fettered and sometimes handcuffed for the next five years. By his own account, his early days in the imposing red-brick prison in Changchun were marked by restlessness, argument, lack of co-operation, and repeated testing of the rules. His trial before the People's Court came 14 months later and, in spite of all that had gone before, he harboured a 'Dream of the Red Mansion' that he would be released. Alas, it was to be a dream unfulfilled, for the court sentenced him, in January 1953, to life imprisonment. It was no use his lodging an appeal, he decided: the charges were trumped up and trivial and it was clear that neither reason nor justice would have any power to reverse the decision.

Resentment and bitterness come through strongly as Duan describes the treatment he received from February 1951 when he was arrested until the eve of his arrival at Fushun in September 1956. He was particularly offended that in prison he should be cheek-by-jowl with the riff-raff of Chinese society: former gamblers, prostitutes and members of underground societies – all outlawed by the new control. How deplorable, he thought, that Guomindang personnel should be mixed in with these! There could be no justifiable comparison between the two groups: with honourable intention the Guomindang had been fighting unselfishly for 30 years for the prosperity of China, while these others had thought of no one but themselves.

From his sentence until mid-1955, Duan made bricks as a member of a 'reform through labour' team, and then all long-term prisoners were withdrawn from these teams. Shortly after, his shackles were removed and other signs of a new treatment policy followed. He and a small group of others of high rank were transferred first to the Jilin province detention centre and then to the Liaoning province detention centre at Shenyang, where they found the living quarters rather cramped. This was not for long though. One day in September 1956 they were assembled and told that, by special approval of State Council, they were to be transferred to a much better prison 40km away at Fushun.

Duan's description of the Fushun prison, its organization and its activities corroborates information received from other sources, though in his comments and assessments he oscillates between praise and cynicism. He speaks well of the cleanliness, appearance and general layout of the prison and praises the cadres for their courtesy, their efforts directed at generating a relaxed atmosphere and the way they played down their role as warders. There was almost no overt supervision even during work outside the prison walls. They got the best out of prisoners by example and encouragment. They not only joined in with manual labour (the first cadres to do so in Duan's experience), but took the lead and set the pace with their own efforts. At harvest and hoeing times in the rice fields the officers selected the more distant and more difficult terrain for themselves and took pride in showing that, even so, they could accomplish more, person for person, than the prisoners. Not that they wished to bully their charges into more work than that for which they were fit. They would actually take over from prisoners who were having difficulty in carrying their shoulder loads. This method of 'silent education' impressed Duan. At play also the cadres encouraged the prisoners to diversify their activities, showing them, for example, how to improvise a skating rink in winter. Jin Yuan, in the beginning a section chief promoted later to commandant, is singled out for special approbation as a cadre who was capable, conscientious and responsible and who had a way of winning people's affection. According to Duan, everyone addressed him as Director (*zhuren*) and respected him as an expert in thought reform.

But not all of Duan Kewen's narration is warm in its recollection. Just as he himself in his frustration was given to periodic outbursts of anger, so his writing is punctuated with passages in which resentment overcomes admiration, and he makes some bitter attacks on the prison personnel. At the cadres' suggestion, inmates constructed a greenhouse in one corner of the prison grounds with the expectation of supplementing their winter diet. Instead, their food ration was reduced. (This coincided with the famine years of the late fifties.) No doubt the cadres and the Japanese prisoners benefited, writes Duan. At another time, they set up a poultry run and were producing 400 eggs a day, but none of these turned up in the meals of the Guomindang prisoners. Duan surmises cynically that they went to the cadres themselves or perhaps to the favoured Manchu prisoners. Even more favoured than the Manchus were the Japanese who were treated with meticulous care, and when all of them were set free ahead of Guomindang prisoners, Duan railed against the irony of releasing men who had butchered Chinese while continuing to incarcerate fellow Chinese.

The tours, too, came under criticism in one of Duan's articles. Although he enjoyed them, he writes sceptically of some aspects. An advanced flax mill visited in Harbin had been built, not by the Communists, but by the Russians before them. A reservoir near Fushun had been designed by the Russians and it was forced labour that completed the construction. A family into whose home he was invited lived pretty well and this impressed him until he found out that the head of the family had been a rich peasant and that the son was a Communist Party cadre. The flats in a new workers' village near Shenyang were, on the other hand, cramped and lacking in lifts, and tenants had to share toilets. Of the various families they visited they were expected to ask pardon for their former crimes. Duan drew the line at kneeling in humility before them — he merely squatted.

Duan was especially incredulous of the large number of crimes confessed to by his colleagues. Of 10,000 criminal items listed by some 300 men, he is sure that 99 per cent were invented.

More than once, Duan refers to himself as having been a difficult person. He boasts in fact of having been more unccooperative than anyone else. He certainly did not align himself with those of his associates who were prepared to be chosen as team leaders and the like. They were but yes-men for the administration in his view.

In summary, then, by no stretch of the imagination could Duan Kewen be regarded as a 'reformed' person by the time of the final release of war criminals in 1975. He remained antagonistic to his captors, to the Communist Party and to the new government. Because of this, his testimony serves us well. The strong vein of scepticism running through his articles adds credibility to his documentation of organization and events in the prison and the factual information he provides has been drawn on to supplement other sources in the description that follows in the next chapter. As to his evaluative comments, at least when they are favourable, we can accept them as having substance.

10 FUSHUN PRISON

> Let a ruler base his government upon virtuous principles.
> (*Analects of Confucius*, II, 1.)

By train from Peking to Fushun is an overnight journey lasting until noon the next day. It is not to be recommended in the depth of a northern winter to anyone who might wish to combine sightseeing with bodily comfort. But on our mission – a visit to the former Fushun war criminals control centre – the approach at this time of year did not seem inappropriate. First light revealed a bleak, chill, uninviting landscape, bringing to mind the film setting of 'One Day in the Life of Ivan Denisovitch'. It seemed that some of the outside world penetrated the double glazing of our compartment – some of the cold for certain in spite of the train's heating system, but also the atmosphere. The thought of a prison is chilling enough at any time. How much the more in this setting! To add a sinister touch, the railway line is still flanked in this part of the world, especially as one nears Shenyang (Mukden), by numbers of pillboxes, reminders of a confused half century before Liberation: of Japanese occupation, of the kingdom of Manzhouguo, of Russian invasion, of civil war.

Fushun is some 50km beyond Shenyang. A city of well over a million inhabitants, it is a major coal-producing centre. Enormous reserves of coal are here. Even under the Japanese, production reached ten million tons a year. Now it must be nearer twenty million, the open cut presenting as a huge scar on the landscape. The engineering industries of the city specialize in the manufacture of heavy machinery, and atmospheric pollution is all too noticeable. The surrounding plains are fertile enough, but the growing season is so short and the winter so long that Liaoning province has to import grain to augment its own harvest.

The Fushun prison – from 1950 to 1975 strictly known as the Fushun War Criminals' Administration Centre (*Fushun zhanfan guanlisuo*) is a single-storied building, the administration section at the front being surmounted by an observation tower rising to 12m or so. When we first saw it on 15 January, the entrance portico sported a banner celebrating the new year. In odd juxtaposition to this welcome, there stood in the shadows of the portico a public security guard with bayonet fixed to his rifle. Although this building has not, since 1975,

56

been used to house war criminals, about one-half of it is still used today as an ordinary prison. It was originally erected by the Japanese army as an officers' prison.

At the entrance we were received by the present governor of the prison, Liu Qinshi, and ushered into the somewhat faded and forbidding reception room of the administration section. Here, plied with the inevitable and never-failing tea, we engaged in interviews over the next two-and-a-half days with prison personnel, the most significant of whom for our purposes was Jin Yuan. Jin is now Deputy Director of the Bureau of Citizen Affairs for the city of Fushun and is no longer a prison officer, but he was for many years on the staff of Fushun prison and rose to be its commandant for several of those years up to 1975. He is a member of the Korean national minority, he is intelligent, smart of appearance, and possessed of a lively sense of humour. He treated us to a well-organized description of the prison from his point of view with particular reference to its educational programme. His account is set out later in this chapter.

We also interviewed five other prison officers, still employed by Public Security, who had been on the staff of the prison with Jin Yuan and who had taken part in the re-education of war criminals. These were Wang Daojian, Liu Jiachang, Zhang Weizhou (medical officer), Sun Shiqiang and Cai Zhicheng. During the two-and-a-half days of discussion and over dinner, they recollected for us what they remembered of Huang Wei, Pujie and Hu Yunhong, and told us something of themselves and their methods. A couple of brief self-portraits will suggest the way these men saw themselves and their task.

Sun Shiqiang was born in 1932 and took up the position of tutor when the Fushun prison was set up in 1950. He was then 18 years of age and had had only six years of schooling. Like most of the tutors he came from the less privileged sector of the old society. (An exception, he pointed out, was the doctor, Zhang Weizhou. Zhang was the only one on the staff who had had more than a junior high school education.) When he started, Sun was not very happy at the thought of being mixed up with criminals, but he came to see the job as an important one, though certainly not an easy one. It needed a lot of preparation and he studied hard within the Party organization. He mentioned that he was well known to Pujie (whom we had already met in Peking) and formerly to the late Puyi. He had had long and close contact with both; but no (in answer to our question) he was not overawed by 'paper tigers', in spite of his lack of formal education.

Wang Daojian was born in 1931 and started at Fushun in 1957.

Before that he had served in the People's Liberation Army and in the police force. With only five years of formal education behind him he had difficulty, for he knew that he would need to acquire a fair under-standing of Marxism-Leninism-Mao Zedong Thought. However he was encouraged by the confidence shown in him by the government and the Party in sending him to Fushun and he determined to try to do the job well. One of the first things he did on arriving at Fushun was to start reading the dossiers on individual prisoners. Seeing accounts of some of their atrocities he could not be happy with the policy of the Party towards these criminals. He could not see the point of trying to reform them. Why bother with the Japanese, for example? And why be so lenient towards them? Besides, could work with criminals qualify as 'serving the people'? As he progressed more and more deeply into his study of Marxism-Leninism-Mao Zedong Thought and of Party policy, he came to understand that the practice proposed agreed with the theory. Party policy was to eliminate class distinctions and the reform of prisoners was a step in this direction. He then accepted that all people could be reformed and he wanted to learn the methods to be used in reforming war criminals. In working out their techniques, the tutors drew to some extent on the experience of the Red Army in dealing with captured Nationalist soldiers.

During our stay in Fushun, we made two inspections of a sub-stantial portion of the prison buildings and we were able to relate these inspections to a detailed plan we were permitted to examine from government records. We were not permitted to photograph the plan, but the dimensions shown on the sketch (Figure 10.1) were taken from the official plan and the layout was checked by actual inspection. It is useful to relate a summary history of the prison to this ground plan.

The Fushun centre was established in July 1950 with six sections, numbered as in the sketch. 1,062 Japanese war prisoners were housed in sections 2, 3, 4, 5 and 6 with a living area of 1,969 sq. m. This averages at 1.85 sq. m. per person. Generals and other high-ranking officers occupied the rooms in divisions 5 and 6, other ranks occupied divisions 2, 3 and 4. The Japanese prisoners comprised members of the expeditionary forces stationed to the east of the gateway in the Great Wall at Shanhaiguan – the so-called Guandong Army – together with military personnel who had been in control of the Puyi regime in Manzhouguo. Division 1 was reserved for the former emperor, his ministers, the governors of the Manchu provinces and high level commanders-in-chief under his puppet government.

Figure 10.1: The War Criminals' Administration Centre, Fushun, Liaoning Province

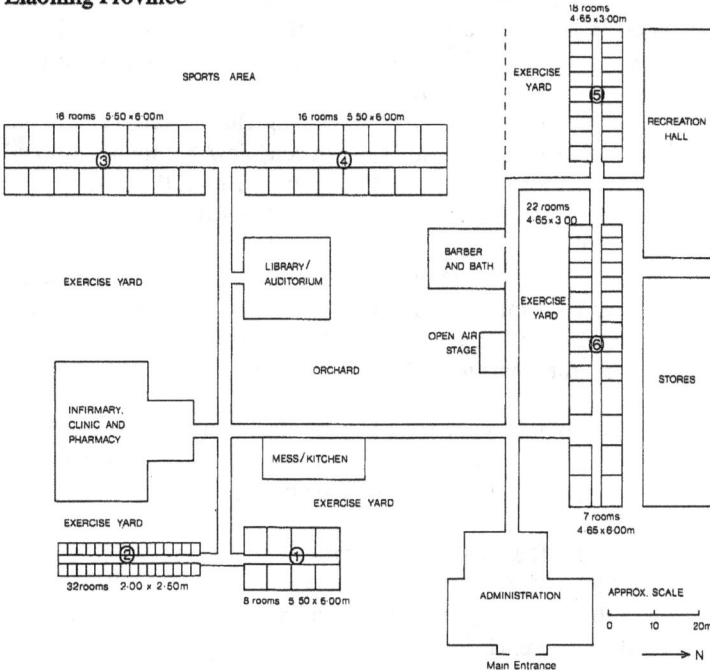

This was the situation until mid-1956 when 1,017 Japanese war prisoners were released and repatriated. The 45 remaining Japanese were moved to the hospital area in the southern part of the prison and sections 5 and 6 were assigned to ordinary prisoners. The Manchu prisoners remained in section 1. This release of the majority of Japanese cleared the way for the gathering together of a number of Guomindang war criminals from various parts of China. By late 1956, sections 3 and 4 were occupied by these Guomindang men. They had come mainly from the armed forces and public security forces and from among government and party officials. Some had been captured in battle and some had been arrested by the new local security agencies. A further rearrangement was made in 1958 when the Manzhouguo prisoners were mixed in with the Guomindang contingent. Sections 1 and 2 were from then on allocated to manual and vocational work.

December 1959 saw the beginning of the release of Manchu and Guomindang prisoners from Fushun and other prisons. On this occasion, the emperor Puyi was released. Further releases were made in

1960, 1961 and 1963, and the remaining Japanese were repatriated in 1964. From 1964 there were still about 300 Guomindang personnel in Fushun. It is not clear how many of the 57 war criminals released at the sixth amnesty in April 1966 were from Fushun, but from then until 1975 there were no more releases. From late 1967, a further number of Guomindang prisoners (including Huang Wei) were moved to Fushun from Peking's Qin Cheng prison, now becoming crowded following arrests associated with the Cultural Revolution. About this time, too, the prison came under military administration for a year or so, and the public security staff were sent off for the time being to the countryside. During the last few years leading up to the final amnesty, section 3 was used for recreation purposes while those needing special care — the aged and the ill — were housed in the hospital area. In March 1975, the remaining 293 war criminals were pardoned and released.

The prison routine was described in outline by former commandant Jin Yuan as follows. A single daily routine was established for the three categories of prisoner. The winter time-table went this way:

0600–0700	Rise, wash, clean quarters
0700–0800	Physical exercises, breakfast
0800–1200	Study sessions (3½ hours with recess 1000–1030)
1200–1300	Lunch
1300–1600	Manual labour
1600–1700	Supper
1700–2100	Recreational activities and free time
2100	Retire.

In food, the prisoners' living standard was no lower than that of the population at large. Staple was rice and flour, including 15 per cent rough grain (for example millet). The monthly quota of pork was 2½kg, of fish 5kg and of eggs 2½kg. Fresh vegetables were available in season. The daily calorie intake was 2,500–3,000. The prisoners' diet was in fact better than that of the working staff. Every week there would be some treat in the way of dumplings and the like, and at festival times (for example, New Year) there would be additional supplies of sweets and fruit. Clothing was supplied free in summer and winter as appropriate. Daily items, such as towels and toothbrushes were supplied according to need, as were study items like paper, notebook and pens. Health was carefully attended to. Each prisoner was given an annual check-up by senior medical officers from Shenyang.

Minor illnesses were looked after in the camp, and for more serious illnesses prisoners were admitted either to the Fushun city hospital or the provincial hospital in Shenyang. There were regular dental and optical attention, and spectacles were provided where needed. There were some cases of serious illness for which the prisoner was permitted to stay with his family to ensure proper care. There were regular inoculations and prisoners were encouraged in matters of personal hygiene. There was no major outbreak of an infectious disease or of food poisoning in the 25 years of the prison's existence. The library (the building marked as library on the sketch was, when we saw it, equipped as a small theatre with proscenium stage and an auditorium with 135 chairs neatly arranged) contained books on history, literature, society and the economy. Towards the end of the period there were over ten thousand volumes (many in Japanese) and prisoners were allowed to borrow them. Periodicals were also available, such as the *People's Daily*, the *Liaoning Daily* and pictorials. Speakers were frequently invited to give talks to the prisoners. Sometimes it was Jin himself talking on current events, both domestic and international, sometimes it was a staff tutor or someone from outside, like a model worker or Party expert. The sons and daughters of war prisoners were sometimes invited in to tell about recent developments and to encourage their fathers to reform. Recreational activities were varied. Every week there was a film session, and television was available every evening. In the summer, prisoners organized stage performances among themselves, such as Peking opera, plays, cross-talk, and presented them on the open-air platform set at one end of what is now an orchard. They learnt revolutionary songs and played violin, flute, drums and piano accordion. Before breakfast and at recess times there were physical exercises performed to music, and organized games included basketball, volley ball, ping pong, chess, go and board games. Two sports meetings were held each year, one in the spring and one in the autumn. The Japanese were fond of holding open-air parties in the central courtyard during summer weeks. In the later years of the prison especially, as the prisoners got older, many of the Chinese men wanted to take up *taijiquan*, so instructors were brought in to teach them. Hot baths were supplied once a week in winter and twice a week in summer. Cold baths were available at any time. (The bath house when we saw it contained two deep concrete baths, each nearly 6m long and 3m wide, and one long wash trough.) Prisoners could have a shave at the barber's shop every two weeks and a haircut once a month. There was a steam laundry for bedclothes and utensils, and bedding had to be aired in the sun weekly.

Having given this outline of the prison regimen, Jin Yuan then spoke at length about the educational programme; for, as he saw it, the prison was not just a place where criminals were rounded up, but a place of education adhering to Chairman Mao's principle that every person is capable of being reformed. Thus, said Jin, was the method of reprisal abandoned.

A Prison Commandant Recalls

Jin Yuan, when he heard that we were coming and that we had a special interest in educational policy and practice, made an effort to recollect his time at the prison. He organized his account in five sections: (1) Basic policies and general conditions in the prison camp; (2) The first stage of re-education: admitting one's crimes; (3) Education through tours; (4) Education through labour; (5) Education in revolution using humane principles. The following is what he had to say.

(1) Basic Policies and General Conditions

The camp admitted three categories of prisoner — three mountains oppressing the masses: Japanese, Manchu government officials and Guomindang personnel. The establishment of the Manzhouguo regime under the control of the Japanese brought disaster to this part of China. The Japanese adopted a policy of triple atrocity (*san guang zhengce*), a policy of burn all, kill all, loot all. Such was the severity of this policy that a single Japanese commander could, during the course of his command, be responsible for killing 40,000 people and burning 20,000 houses. According to the confessions made by the 1,000 or so Japanese prisoners themselves, between them they killed more than 940,000 Chinese people and burned more than 480,000 houses. As a result of the Japanese invasion, more than 12 million lives were lost and 50 thousand million dollars' worth of property destroyed, not including property looted. Not only the Japanese, but also Chiang Kai-shek's clique pursued a policy of death and destruction. They believed it better to kill 1,000 innocent people than to let a single communist party member go free. The Guomindang prisoners in the camp, between them, confessed to more than 40,000 criminal acts.

Had we adopted a reprisals policy (continued Jin) these crimes could never have been redeemed even by execution. Instead, the Chinese

Communist Party adopted a liberal policy, one that would be of benefit to the Chinese people, the Party and the world revolutionary cause. To have executed these people would have been easier than to reform them; but the decision to reform was a step towards the realization of Marxist-Leninist theories and of Mao Zedong Thought leading to the extinction of class and the eventual setting up of a Communist society. It was also a form of realization of the character of China and its people.

The re-education policy adopted could be typified as a combination of punishment with leniency, reform through labour with political education, and class struggle with revolutionary aim. It was hard for the prison staff to carry out this reform policy properly, for their own families and friends in many cases had suffered at the hands of the Japanese and the Guomindang. In the early days of the programme, when the staff saw that the prisoners were on better rations than they themselves, it was quite common for the cook not to be particular about washing the rice properly, nor the barber to worry about hair style. Even the medical staff would give only desultory service. Not approving of the kind of reform methods being instituted, some of the workers in the prison would have preferred transfer to other posts.

A prerequisite then to the success of the programme was that the prison workers should themselves be re-educated. In fact, none of them was allowed to transfer, but all were encouraged to study Chairman Mao's works and some of the relevant Party instructions, for example, those issuing from the second (1949) plenary session of the seventh Central Committee, relating to the transfer of emphasis from rural to urban areas. (This was a very significant session coming on the eve of the Communists' nation-wide victory and defining many of the policies to be followed in establishing a socialist society. See Mao Zedong's report to the session in *SW*, IV: 361-75.)

A story illustrates nicely how the staff came to see the importance of their own attitude in producing the desired changes in that of the prisoners. One prison worker had had two brothers killed by the Japanese. One day in the camp he was subjected to an insult by an arrogant Japanese officer prisoner. Knowing the rules, he retired to his own room to fret alone and said nothing in retort. Two or three days later he was insulted again by the same man. This time, not able to bear it in silence, he blurted out, 'My two brothers were killed by you Japanese and now I have to bear your insults because of our Party's policy.' As word of the incident spread among the Japanese prisoners there was a noticeable change of atmosphere. The prison workers too began to see that their job of reforming the prisoners was a continuation of the work done by the soldiers who had captured the Japanese on the battlefield: a worthwhile next step in the revolutionary cause.

There was one occasion when a staff member, still doubting the reform policy, approached the commandant to request interviews with Premier Zhou Enlai and Chairman Mao to confirm it. However, the staff gradually came round to accepting the measures that had been instituted for these Japanese prisoners.

When the Guomindang prisoners began to arrive in 1956, after most of the Japanese had been sent home, there was again some reluctance on the part of the staff to extend the reform policy to these men. By this time, however, the staff had had more experience and came round fairly quickly.

Indeed, it was not only those members of staff in direct daily contact with the prisoners who demonstrated the desired attitudes, but the support staff as well. For example, one day a group of Guomindang prisoners had stripped while working in a field some seven or eight *li* from the camp, and had left their clothes in a pile at the edge of the field. When it began to rain, a woman typist took off her own raincoat and used it to protect the prisoners' clothes. The prisoners found their clothes dry, while she was wet through.

On another occasion, one of the prisoners had to be transferred ill to a hospital in the city. One of the camp medical officers accompanied him. Finding that the patient needed to be taken to the third floor and there being no carrying facilities available because it was the middle of the night, the officer himself carried the patient pick-a-back — an action that moved the patient to tears.

Then again, the staff in charge of ordering camp supplies took a hand in the re-education programme. Knowing how averse to manual labour many of the prisoners would be, the supply staff tried to find articles (for example, crockery) bearing slogans in praise of labour: 'To labour is glorious', 'History is possible because of the working people', etc. (Cf. 'Cherish manual labour, hold manual labour in respect, understand that the working people are the makers of history of mankind and that without manual labour there will be no mankind and no history of mankind. — *Renmin Xuexi Cidian* (A Study Phrase-book for the People), Shanghai, 1953: 325.)

Along with changes in the attitude of the staff came gradual changes in the attitude of the prisoners. For example, in the early days it was fairly common for Japanese prisoners to address a camp officer by some nickname. This gradually gave way to calling him by function (e.g., platoon leader), then 'tutor', and finally 'Mr Tutor'.

By 1956, recognizing the success of the reform policy, the government decided not to proceed to the court martial of the majority of the Japanese prisoners, but instead released them. On their release they were given new shoes, clothes, Russian-style blankets and $100 for buying souvenirs. The prisoners were released in three batches and returned by ship from Tianjin. As they took their leave, they presented the Chinese with souvenir banners expressing their gratitude for the leniency of the government and expressing their wish to devote themselves to the eventual peace of the world. At a final celebratory banquet there were embraces between Japanese and the Chinese staff of the prison. Among the remaining 45 Japanese prisoners who were court martialled, some were given sentences of 20 years and others lesser sentences down to 13 years. In 1964, when some had come to the end of their sentence, all in fact were released.

Of the Guomindang prisoners, some were released in 1959, the tenth anniversary of the founding of the People's Republic. Altogether six batches, numbering a total of 296 prisoners, were released in the period 1959-66. After 1966, the climate of the Cultural Revolution prevented any further amnesties until 1975 when, at the instigation of Chairman Mao and with the approval of the National People's Congress, all remaining 293 were released.

There were three cardinal principles governing the release of the Chinese prisoners. First they must admit their crimes, then they must give their support to the socialist system, and lastly they must wholeheartedly support the Chinese Communist Party, its representatives and its policies as well as the government's policies and the legal code.

The first recommendation as to who should be included in an amnesty would come from the tutors who would then canvass opinions from among the prisoners themselves. These recommendations would then go to the Liaoning provincial branch of the Party where the recommendations would be discussed by executive members of the Party. After their approval, the recommendations would pass through Public Security to the Central Committee of the Party. None of the recommendations originating from the prison staff was rejected at upper levels (to his knowledge, Jin qualified) a reflection of the thoroughness with which staff sought unanimous agreement among themselves in the first place.

When Chinese prisoners were released, they would be allocated jobs by the united front organization at various levels (*Renmin zhengzhi xieshang huiyi*: People's Political Consultative Conference). The prison authorities assisted the organization in this matter, particularly alerting it to any prisoner needing special help in respect of health or finance.

After the Japanese returned to their home country, most of them became helpful citizens. Some wrote books arising out of their experiences in China with titles such as *The Three Olds, Aggression, The Soldiers of the Japanese Emperor* and *The Road We Have Travelled*. The returned Japanese formed an organization with many branches throughout Japan and each year hold a convention. In recent years there have been six occasions when delegates from this association have revisited China and on each occasion they have returned to Fushun. The Japanese in fact regard Fushun as the place of their rebirth and consider the staff of the prison as the benevolent mentors of their reform. (It has been part of the Japanese military ethic to die rather than surrender to the enemy. To regard imprisonment metaphorically as a period of rebirth may be a way of rationalizing survival in the face of this ethic.)

Among the Manchu prisoners, the most successful reform case was that of Henry Puyi, the former Emperor. He became an expert in horticulture. The book he eventually published after his release was written here in prison (Aisin-Gioro Pu Yi, 1964-5). After release he foreswore his former life style and was grateful that he could now support himself by his own work. There are many stories of his new-found humility and modesty. One of these relates to when he was living with some relatives shortly after release and he volunteered to sweep the nearby streets. He became so absorbed that he was lost and had to ask his way back home. On other occasions, going shopping with his sister, he would act so retiringly at the bus stop allowing others to to board first that the bus-driver would sometimes imagine that he did not want to catch the bus. The bus would move off separating him from his sister who would then have to alight at the following stop to wait. His first regular job was in the Shangshan botanical gardens in Peking. While working there he often saw militia units training and expressed a desire to join in with them. He was refused at first because of his age, but later was given permission. Following his gardens post, he was reassigned to work in the archives of the Political Consultative Conference.

There are many stories too of the exemplary behaviour of Guomindang prisoners after release. One who was assigned to factory work was elected as 'model worker' eleven times. Some refused to accept their wages, preferring instead to establish a fund to help in the reconstruction of the country. An example of real success in vocational training is that of the ex-prisoner who went to work in a production brigade looking after orchards. He did so well that he was promoted to working as a horticultural specialist at county level.

It is important to note that all the Chinese who were released were granted citizenship. (This was contradicted by a Hong Kong journalist who told the author that he believed at least one general released in 1975 remained without full citizen rights and was under supervision.) Those who could work were given employment, those who were sick were given medical care. As for cadres, those too old to work were granted a pension, and those who wanted to migrate to Taiwan were given a travelling allowance together with the opportunity of returning to China. All received new clothing and $100 pocket money. On release they were received by Party and government leaders at banquets and they were also taken on visits so as to acquire first-hand acquaintance with the latest developments. Ten who applied to go to Taiwan took their travelling allowances and went to Hong Kong to await their visas. Visas were refused and, in this refusal, the Taiwan clique showed their fear of the truth. The Communist rulers have no such fear of truth. (Cai Xingsan, an interview with whom is reported in Chapter 8, was one of these ten. So also was Duan Kewen whose autobiographical articles, published by *Shijie Ribao* (*World Journal*) in New York were used in evidence by Amnesty International in its report; see Chapter 9.)

(2) Admitting One's Crimes

To admit crimes is the first and most important step in the re-education programme. Nothing can be done until this is accomplished. It is not an easy thing for any people to change their fundamental ideology, more particularly for the middle-aged and old.

The Japanese war prisoners did not think they had committed any crime. They worshipped their Emperor who could do no wrong. They possessed the spirit of Great Japan and held to the Samurai tradition. They believed they were superior to all other Asians and all other races. They believed Japan's entry into the Second World War was a matter of survival, necessitated by a large population in a restricted territory. If any admission of crime was necessary, then surely nothing more was called for than their nation's acknowledgement by the act of surrender in 1945.

As for the Manchus, their attitude may be seen by considering Puyi. Henry Puyi believed that he was the Son of Heaven with a duty to rule his people. His co-operation with the Japanese had been a righteous bid to restore the dynasty and so achieve his duty. He saw no wrong here. It will be recalled that on the surrender of the Japanese the Russians captured the Manchu court and took them to Moscow. There they continued to live in palace style. Puyi had with him a brother (Pujie — see Chapter 6), two brothers-in-law, three nephews and one attendant, all of whom still addressed him as 'Imperial Majesty'. Henry lived upstairs while his relatives lived below. If sometimes he felt displeased he would have his relatives come up and parade before him and then kneel down in two facing rows and hit each other. He was thus still permitted self-indulgence. In 1950 when Puyi was sent back to China he was clearly frightened. It is reported that when he was met at the border he kept reiterating, 'I am the last emperor of the Manchu dynasty; I am the kindest of persons; I have never killed a living thing.' He showed some signs of mental disorder. When he and his entourage (the total group of ministers and family numbered about 60) came to Shenyang by train, they were met by officials from the North-East Public Security who conducted them to a reception hall where there were fruit, cigarettes, lemonade and tea. Puyi immediately rushed in to eat as much water-melon as possible, evidently believing this may be his last meal. So busy was he that he could not attend to what was being said.

The Guomindang group did not consider that they had committed crimes either. They claimed that they had held their posts according to the constitution and that therefore their actions were legal. They were, what is more, followers of Dr Sun Yat-sen. They also accused the Communists of being rebels and bandits and claimed that Marxist-Leninism was not suited to Chinese needs. They believed that their failure was but a temporary one brought on by some mistakes in the leadership of Chiang Kai-shek.

In all, the prisoners were firm in the opinion that they had committed no crimes. They invented all sorts of justifications for their actions. It was thus a difficult task to re-educate them.

Take the case of the Japanese again. These prisoners had been detained in Russia for five years where no attempt had been made to re-educate them. They had undergone hard labour, constructing roads and building houses. When they were handed over to the Chinese in July 1950, one Russian officer offered the opinion that these were hard core Japanese — one could not expect to reform them. To reform or not is an example of the debate between the two lines. (The two lines (*liangtiao luxian*) are the contrasting ones of socialist construction and Right opportunism.) In the end, Chairman Mao's instruction was followed and an attempt at reform instituted. But it was a demanding undertaking. The Japanese would shout slogans frequently: 'Long live the Japanese Emperor!', 'Long live Japanese imperialism!' Every morning they bowed ceremoniously to the East. They acted in a superior manner to the Chinese on whom they looked down as inferior. Most of them refused to read any of the newspapers offered and they covered their ears against the broadcasting. There was one prisoner in particular, something of a hero among his own colleagues, who kept shouting, 'I want my freedom; if you want to kill me, kill me, but don't otherwise deprive me of my freedom!' Encouraged by his colleagues, this man became more and more violent. Rather than punish him, it was decided to try to persuade him to a different point of view. He was brought in for private sessions. At first he refused to sit down when offered a seat but persisted in his claim that the Chinese had no right to imprison him. The Japanese had been sent by their Emperor and thus had only been doing their duty. He himself had been a police officer assisting the Manzhouguo government with internal security. In any case, he had come before the Communist take-over, so what right did the Communists have to imprison him? Prison officers reasoned with him, pointing out that no forces invading another country could be regarded as guiltless. As the reasoning proceeded he began to fall silent, and it was then put to him that, now that he saw he was not standing on reason, he should write a self-examination report. His first such report was only a few words. Not until his fourth attempt was it accepted by staff. He was then asked to tell his colleagues about his crimes, but, because he was such a hero in their eyes, he did not see how he could do this. He requested time to think over the matter and a week later consented. His broadcast over the public address system was in a low voice, but because of his standing he had the attention of all. In this way the internees came round to the view that it was better not to be discourteous or to misbehave lest they get into trouble. From that time on (about January 1951) the shouting of slogans and bowing to the East gradually disappeared. Of course these were not necessarily signs of inward reform, but only a first step — conformity to avoid trouble. It was, in addition, an interesting demonstration of how one person might be used as an example to bring about a change in all.

Another example to illustrate the step of admitting crimes is the case of Henry Puyi. At first when Henry was brought to the prison camp he lived in the one room with his relatives. He needed help in such elementary matters as dressing himself. The staff decided that as long as he was permitted to remain so dependent the chance of reform would be dismal. So they separated him from his relatives, ignoring his cries for help. Over a period of four months, then, the re-education of Henry's relatives was intensified, and then came a breakthrough. One of the nephews let out the information that when Henry had left the Imperial Palace in the 1930s to go to Tianjin under the protection of the Japanese he had taken with him some very valuable antiques secretly stowed in a steel trunk measuring 1m × 800cm × 500cm. This trunk accompanied him when he became puppet Emperor of Manzhouguo and later went with him to Russia, returning with him to China. No one ever suspected that it contained anything more than clothes. Now that the nephew had revealed his uncle's secret, he hoped that the authorities would confiscate the valuables. Instead the prison staff decided to wait patiently until Henry himself volunteered the information after recognizing his guilt. Two more months went by and the nephew, becoming impatient, left an anonymous note for Henry recommending he confess. This led Henry to request, out of fear, a private interview during the course of which he told how he had brought with him these priceless items and he now thought he should turn them over to the government. The tutor's reply was that for the moment they should be regarded as Henry's private property and simply stored for him. Whether or not they should belong to the people was something that could be decided later. After this interview Henry believed he would probably receive more accusations and criticisms of his behaviour. On the contrary he was praised for having done something meritorious. He was much moved by this. Incidents like this were very important, for through them, the internees learned that to reveal one's thoughts brought leniency. Henry was happy to reveal the story to his entourage.

Over a period of about a year when prisoners began admitting their crimes, the authorities on their side were collecting evidence from people who had been directly affected by these crimes. This information was not disclosed to the prisoners but was kept by the prison authorities and used by them as a means of verifying the prisoners' confessions. This mobilization of people outside the prison to assist can be regarded as an aspect of the 'mass line'. Prisoners were also encouraged to inform against each other and such informing often provided the basis for one's own confession. By the end of the first year most of the war criminals had admitted their crimes in honest confession.

An example of this second step in the process of admitting crimes is that of a Japanese Major-General who was very reluctant to confess.

Twenty of his junior officers were in the prison. They admitted their part in civilian killings and in the burning of houses and, one by one, they began accusing the Major-General also. He said at first that he had no knowledge of these crimes: 'If you carried out these crimes without my knowledge, then I was not a good commander; that was my only wrong. Certainly it is immoral of you to blame all this on me, saying they were my crimes too.' After three days of 'wage a struggle by reasoning' sessions (*jinxing shuoli douzheng hui*), with his juniors giving evidence of the Major-General himself being involved in the crimes, he found there was no escape from admission.

Altogether it took about three years for the prisoners to confess their crimes, report among themselves and have evidence collected and checked. But the process was completed for all 45 of the Japanese who were under sentence. This was in contrast to the results of the Nuremberg trials and the Allied Far Eastern trials.

The third step for the prisoners in this process of crime admission education is that of criticizing and comparing one another's confessions, examining the results of them, and working out a plan to reform themselves.

By 1954 all three steps had been thoroughly carried out among the Japanese and Manchu officers. As for the Guomindang prisoners who were admitted to the prison late in 1956, their crimes were becoming clearer by the end of 1958 — so much so that it was said among the Guomindang prisoners themselves that 'in 1948 we lost the battle of arms; by 1958 we lost also the battle of thoughts'. So as to intensify understanding, the prisoners were encouraged to write autobiographical accounts. These would help the whole world understand too. At length all joined in and some 700 or 800 pieces of work were produced in many different forms — memoirs, plays, poems, essays and fiction. A few of the titles were 'The first half of my life', 'Arson', 'Assassination', 'Concentration camps', 'A living hell', 'A prosecutor's confession' and 'Experiments in germ warfare'. Public readings were arranged and some of these recitals were very moving and proved thereby to be a way of intensifying the re-education process.

(3) Education Through Tours

Because the Guomindang prisoners had been isolated from society for so long, the prison staff considered that organized tours to acquaint them with developments would be an essential part of their re-education. Certainly, outsiders had been brought in to give accounts — family members, experts, even former prisoners — but this was not enough to be convincing. Nor was it sufficient simply to pay visits to the immediate vicinity of Fushun. After all, the north-east had been under Japanese rule for some time and it may well be thought by the prisoners that the rest of China had not kept pace in its industrial reconstruction. Nor would they easily be convinced that 500 million peasants had accepted collective farming. And what of the attitudes now of the old-style industrialists? Were they satisfied that the new ways are better than the old? Then, too, though they might be impressed with the manner and attitudes of the prison staff, could the prisoners believe that these cadres were in any way representative of those outside? Surely they had been specially selected? Finally, what sort of mass support existed for the new regime? Was it of the kind that would ensure a strong China safe from aggression?

It was against this background of thinking that the tours were arranged to help the prisoners' re-education. It was his belief (said Jin Yuan) that this was an original idea, and one as well suited to ordinary prisoners as to those for whom originally designed.

In 1956, just before the release of most of them, the Japanese war prisoners were taken, in three groups, on a tour of China that included Fushun, Shenyang, Anshan, Tianjin, Peking, Wuhan, Hankou, Shanghai, Nanjing, Changchun and Harbin. Their visits included farming, industry, and research and education institutions. After 1958 there were tours of similar extent for Guomindang and Manchu prisoners. Altogether there were five of these designed to tackle different kinds of doubts.

Sometimes during the tours reports were heard from the sufferers of crimes. One particularly poignant example was when Japanese prisoners met a survivor from the 1932 Pingding Shan incident. (Pingdingshan was a village near Fushun entirely destroyed by a contingent of Japanese on 16 September 1932. The 3,000 inhabitants, mostly miners and peasants and their families, were evacuated by force and massacred nearby and their houses were burnt. This was done in reprisal for suspected complicity between the villagers and Chinese militia forces antagonistic to the Japanese occupation following the Mukden incident. In 1971 the site was excavated and a memorial hall was built over the exposed skeletons.) This survivor had been a five-year-old girl at the time and was now a kindergarten teacher. She still bore stab marks on her body. The Japanese invited her to tell her story and then were so overcome they knelt and wept. They were noticeably slow getting back on the bus and many of them could not eat on returning to camp. Some even requested to be sentenced for the crimes committed by their countrymen. This tour — like some others — had greater effect than had been anticipated. Generally the tours were found to meet their prime purpose, that of convincing of developments. They also helped to intensify the admission of crimes.

(4) Education Through Labour

The programme of education through labour (Jin used *laodong fuwu* (service through labour), a term with much milder connotations than the usual *laodong gaizao*) had two purposes: to reform political thought (*zhengzhi sixiang gaizao*) and to provide vocational training (*laodong jineng*).

All the prisoners were of the kind who had looked down on manual labour in the past. Now it was to be used as a method of reform. It was planned according to the person's age, physical condition and capability, and also with the thought of some future vocational need. Factory labour was arranged for some younger ones, such as the production of small electric motors from raw materials. (The factory was adjacent to the prison building, on the south side.) Older ones who were healthy looked after the orchard and vegetable gardens. Special skills were taken into consideration. For example, Henry Puyi with his interest in pathology and the functioning of Chinese herbal medicines was set to work in the herbal section of the prison clinic; Hu Yunhong worked in the library on summaries and organization because of his calligraphic skill; Pujie helped, along with others, at Japanese-Chinese translations. Some of these former prisoners now work in the Foreign Languages Press (Jin added).

Hands that were once engaged in crime were now busy at productive labour, and there were a number of successes. The electric motors already mentioned were actually used in the building of the Great Hall of the People in Peking and favourable comments were fed back from those who used them. After two years' work in the clinic, Henry Puyi was encouraged to apply for admission to practise as a Chinese herbal doctor. Even though he was not quite good enough, he was given a passing grade at the first examination. With this boost to his confidence he went on to better and better grades, but if his success started to go to his head arrangements were made to have the real marks adjusted down as a way of restraining him.

Of course, in organizing manual labour for the prisoners, the cadres had to take part also in the labour and set an example.

(5) Education in Revolution Using Humane Principles

The principle of exercising humanity throughout the methods of reform underlies the account so far. Here (offered Jin) are a few points by way of summary:

1. It is important to regard the prisoners as human beings and show them respect. One must never resort to abuse or corporal punishment, but encourage the criminals to reform themselves in thought and to grow in working skills.

2. It is important to try to establish good living and learning conditions, so that the prisoners will find it easy to accept and undergo re-education and become useful citizens. During the lean years, conditions were hard for the people at large and even the staff of the prison suffered greatly. [The lean years were 1959-61. Contrast Jin Yuan's account of prison diet with the starvation rations and experimental foods described by Bao Ruowong, 1973.] Even so, they did their best to maintain the prisoners' conditions. Within the camp itself, staff and prisoners had their separate mess halls, but when they were engaged in work in the fields some three kilometres away, they would eat together. On these occasions the prisoners could not fail to see that they had better food than the staff. The prisoners would be treated to 'big grain' [rice], steamed dumplings and pork, while the staff had to be content with millet, rough staple and meagre dishes. With effort, a reasonable standard of living was maintained throughout these years.

3. On admission to the camp, personal belongings amounting to some tens of thousands of items were stored by the authorities. All these belongings, down to the least significant, were returned when the prisoners were released.

With an apology for having had to leave out much of what he had prepared, Jin came to the end of his account. He had given us a whole day, but had perhaps not allowed for the time that would be taken up in translating and in responding to our requests for clarification along the way. Nevertheless there is much to be drawn from this statement, especially when set alongside other accounts, and repeated reference is made to it later in the book when an attempt is made at a comprehensive interpretation. At this point it will also be useful to make a few comments on the statement as it stands.

Jin's manner in telling his story had all the marks of earnestness and sincerity — marks declaring that here was a benevolent and thoughtful person. The prisoners with whom we spoke and who had been under his command lent support to this view and appeared to hold him in high and even affectionate respect. Cai Xingsan has written of him as an experienced leader, one who showed a sincere concern and who was very good at winning people. He mentions that he learned to speak and later to write Japanese very well and that he got close enough to the prisoners to solve quietly many of their personal problems. (Cai, August, 1979: 52-5) That Cai and other former prisoners still feel this way after a lapse of years makes it difficult to explain the relationship in terms of the phenomenon of captive identifying with captor.

Jin evinced pride in the methods that had been developed at Fushun, and the problem for the outsider is to judge how far to believe that pride to be justified. In many respects Jin paints a realistic picture. In the early relations that he depicts between staff and Japanese prisoners, for example, one can readily imagine the superior and arrogant manner that Japanese of the officer class in the imperial army would adopt towards the under-educated, peasant-type 'upstarts' who presumed to stand to them in position of tutor. And one can equally understand the murmurings of discontent among the staff at being expected to show any leniency towards the enemies of their revolution so recently and so gloriously come into its own. These descriptions ring true to the Western ear.

Where doubts and difficulties arise is with what sounds like an excess of *naïveté*. The simple moral tales like the one of the typist and her raincoat and some of the Puyi stories are of the kind that have come to be all too familiar to us in Chinese Communist propaganda, but in Western estimation they do nothing for the credibility of the tale teller. There seems to be no recognition of this on the part of many Chinese. More importantly — or is it an extension of the same *naïveté*? — how are we to judge the frankness with which Jin spoke of parts of the re-education process that many of us would see as quite reprehensible?

. To insist on a confession, repeatedly revised and extended, while at the same time knowing it is often produced simply to conform and to avoid trouble would seem to place too low a value on sincerity, even if this is regarded as a first stage only. To withhold what is believed to be incriminating evidence and not to be satisfied until the supposed offender confesses to it is also reprehensible. This must be objected to on the grounds that it is a procedure holding more risks for the innocent than the guilty. The latter can terminate the process at any time (provided he can guess which of his actions he is being called to account for); in the case of the former the process can go on for ever.

These arguments however are not likely to be conceded by one believing himself to be on the side of right and in possession of the truth. So if there is one major criticism of Jin's statement it is that it lacks humility and a recognition of the possibility that there might be not just one truth but many. If we are to learn anything about education in the widest sense from the interview, this is an important criticism. In its context, it might be unrealistic to expect better. There have been many worse prison programmes. For Jin himself, the criticism does not detract from one's assessment of him as sincere and humane.

11 THE RE-EDUCATION PROGRAMME

> Re-education should be directed at building the future. It entails
>   studying theory,
>   raising consciousness,
>   relating to reality,
>   reforming thoughts.
> > (Nie Zhen, Peking, 1979, personal communication)

In the foregoing accounts there have been references to study groups, tours, confessions, labour and other components of the re-education programme. In this chapter, those accounts will be drawn on to attempt a clear picture of the programme as it must have been in its most highly developed form. It was not identical for all prisons, nor did it remain unchanged throughout the whole period in any one location. It was probably in the Fushun setting, in the several years preceding the onset of the Cultural Revolution, that the method reached its most sophisticated level of development, and it is this example that will be drawn on predominantly.

In its organization and in its routine, the prison was geared to the re-education of its inmates. In the typical case, prisoners were divided up into small teams (*dui*) corresponding usually with sleeping arrangements. Each team had between 10 and 15 members from among whom two leaders were appointed with the sanction of the prison administration. One of these leaders chaired a weekly meeting (*sheng huo hui*) concerned with living conditions, health and the issue of toiletries, clothing, writing paper and cigarettes. This leader also managed the roster of labour duties and he was expected to tackle discipline problems and report on them to the administration. The other leader chaired the team in its daily study sessions (*xiao dui hui*). It was his task to transmit the study plan devised by the prison tutors and to direct its implementation within his team. He was expected to keep notes of each meeting and to make reports to the appropriate tutor. Each tutor or political instructor (*zhidaoyuan*) was responsible for the study programme of several teams (*dui*) and from time to time all his groups would band together to form a larger group (*zu*). On these combined occasions the meeting was chaired by a leader drawn from the ranks of the prisoners and appointed by the authorities. The leader of the *zu* was regarded as the immediate superior of all the *dui* leaders and, besides chairing meetings of the *zu*, acted as an intermediary between the prisoners and the administration in the more important aspects of study and of day-to-day living. At one stage at Fushun a further body was introduced. It was known as the study committee, although it had a wider brief than the name suggests. It came to play a very important role in that all study, all criticism sessions and all sporting activities were conducted under its aegis. It was composed of all the *zu* leaders and some other prisoners as well. One from among the members of the committee was appointed as chairman and two secretaries were also chosen. This was the highest body representative of the prison inmates.

Such was the organization then that the bulk of prisoners, outside of the special handful of prisoner leaders, would perceive the immediate front line of control of all their activities — eating, sleeping, working, studying and playing — as being in the hands of prisoners like themselves. The officers in charge were well aware of the enhanced opportunities for peer-group pressure afforded by this arrangement, and much of their eventual success can be attributed to their subtle exploitation of it. Cadres did their planning behind the scenes, restricted themselves in the main to observation at any team meetings they attended, intervened only in difficult situations and, in so far as they came into contact with the general run of prisoners, exerted their influence through hint, suggestion and example. Their refusal to comment directly on written submissions and other work of the prisoners sometimes disconcerted the latter, but it was a deliberate and effective ploy to throw the responsibility of judgement back on the prisoners themselves.

Very early in their detention, prisoners were required to write an account of their life from childhood on. The understanding was that, until a person brought into the forefront of his consciousness the whole of his past life, he could make no judgement of it and accordingly have no basis for a reformed future. In this matter, as on all occasions when prisoners were called on to declare their thoughts, reluctance to write or speak was met by the objection that a mind cannot be empty. A person who said he could not reflect on his own situation must in fact be harbouring questionable thoughts. In an effort to satisfy the demands for minute detail being placed upon them, some prisoners resorted to invention. It appears, however, that the cadres were skilled in detecting fabrications and actually arranged fact-finding missions to native places and former places of residence in order to check the veracity of accounts. Armed with such information, cadres, without further comment, simply refused to accept incomplete submissions and many a prisoner had to rewrite his autobiography several times before his tutor, by accepting it, indicated his satisfaction with the accuracy and extent of detail. The watchword for tutors in this process was patience even in the face of the frustration and resentment that it generated in many of the prisoners. 'If not today, then tomorrow', they would say, and in the end waiting paid off. Even when the submission was at last accepted, its author looked in vain for a positive word of commendation from his tutor. If he was looking for reward he had to find it in the consummation of the task itself.

With their past life recalled, prisoners then had to make an assessment of it with a view to disowning it (*fouding*). In particular, they had to make an exhaustive list of their crimes. This confession of crimes (*jiaozui*) was a very difficult exercise for many whose past actions — now labelled criminal by their captors — were carried out in the pursuit of what they assessed as their legitimate and patriotic duty. Feelings ran hot, according to several testimonies, and, in the words of one participant, during the small group sessions devoted to the drawing up of the crime lists, the whole of the Fushun prison rang like a mad house with prisoners calling out, banging their fists on the tables and stamping their feet. It is clear that there was considerable group pressure on recalcitrant members to conform to expectations. The same participant made the further observation that, between sessions, all would revert to normal with people laughing and smoking as if nothing unusual had happened.

The crime list was a formal document on which had to be set out specific details such as a clear description of each crime, when it was committed, on whose initiative it was executed, who the victims were and the name, age, position and background of persons who could be called upon to witness. There is a suggestion that teams vied with each other in drawing up lists and the participant already referred to quoted an average of between 30 and 40 criminal acts per person.

If the labelling of certain actions as criminal was difficult, the next step of admitting one's guilt (*renzui*) was even more so. To exchange a former sense of duty for a present genuine sense of guilt called for a deep and fundamental change of heart and mind. In a very real sense, the other elements of the programme (study, labour and tours) were also directed towards bringing about this change over time; nevertheless, besides the long-term gentle approach, some short-term 'shock' techniques were occasionally used. Public confessions and admissions of guilt were staged. One description of a large-scale meeting at the Fushun prison told of how the pattern was deliberately set by having the first two or three confessions declaimed by persons practised in stagecraft and public speaking. With the pattern thus established, others would conquer their timidity and come forward. People who, even so, could not confront the assembly and speak out might be taken aside by two or three of their peers (usually members of the study committee) for a heart-to-heart talk. At one time, in Fushun, a special room for these private talks was set apart and called the *jiaoxin fang* — the room for opening up one's heart — its walls hung with posters depicting crimes belonging to the past. Sometimes, a confession was broadcast over the public address system, especially if it was of a prominent person, in the hope that this might encourage others. All these measures were usually confined to the time-tabled study periods and any pressure was immediately relaxed at the conclusion of a period.

Although there was considerable use of group situations to stimulate conflict, it is clear that the object throughout was to create conflict within the individual himself rather than between individuals, so that each might learn to face up to the contradiction inherent in his own past and in his own allegedly erroneous thoughts.

There is no report of physical coercion being resorted to at Fushun, though Duan Kewen reported that he was confined there for a fortnight to write his confession and that in an earlier prison he had been hand-cuffed and fettered for non-co-operation. This latter assertion was not denied as improbable by the authorities we consulted in Peking.

A central element of the programme, stressed as important by all the Peking and Fushun officials we interviewed and prominent in all the accounts by former prisoners, was the daily study session. These sessions, conducted in the small teams (*dui*), were the means of trans-mitting the facts and ideology that were to be the foundation on which to base a new outlook. The basic texts were newspaper and journal articles, the writings of Chairman Mao (for example, 'On New Democracy', 'On Coalition Government', 'On Practice') and, regarded as most important of all, *The History of the Development of Society* (*Shehui fazhan shi*), a work setting forth the theme that labour created human beings and that wealth and social progress come through the efforts of the labouring classes. These materials gave rise to discussion and essay-writing and were related concretely to events in the prisoners' backgrounds.

The basic discussion technique was that known as 'criticism and self-criticism' (*piping he ziwo piping*), a method developed within the

Communist Party and promoted for use not only by Party members but also by the masses at large. The Central Committee of the Party had launched it publicly as early as April 1950 in a nation-wide effort to raise political consciousness (*RMRB*, 23 April 1950). In the case of war criminals, it was expected that its use would, at the same time as it raised prisoners' consciousness, intensify their guilt for past actions and thoughts. Ideally the ultimate effect of study, criticism and the intensification of guilt was intended to be positive and forward-looking rather than negatively dwelling on the past. Prisoners were encouraged to think about their future and how they might plan it in the context of a socialist China and on the basis of their newly-developed ideology.

But, in any truly Marxist scheme, study, speculation, criticism and planning could never be permitted to stand apart from practice. 'Marxists regard man's activity in production as the most fundamental practical activity, the determinant of all his other activities', wrote Mao ('On Practice', *SW*, I:295-309), and prominent in all Communist rhetoric is that this general principle should have its application in each and every individual. All should have experience of productive manual labour (*laodong*). It is written also into the crime statutes as a means of rehabilitation (*laodong jiaoyang*) and of reform (*laodong gaizao*) for those who have transgressed in action or thought. The high status prisoners with whom this investigation is concerned were no exception to the general rule. Having said that, however, it must be recorded that there is no suggestion that for them labour was imposed punitively. Certainly those who were physically fit in Fushun found themselves tending the vegetable plot, looking after animals and working in the rice fields nearby, but they worked at these agricultural tasks no more energetically than did the cadres who were also conforming to the universal labour rule. The extent to which a prisoner was expected to work was tempered to his age and physical condition and, for some, labour meant little more than applying their calligraphic skill to writing notices or sewing on buttons. The important thing was, as one prison officer said, that hands once engaged in crime were now turned to the good of mankind. For some inmates there were technical skills to be acquired in the workshops attached to the prisons. Fushun had a factory for producing small electric generators, for instance.

To sum up, while participating in labour, prisoners were expected to make progress with their own ideological reform, learning new skills that might assist with their rehabilitation on release and contribute to their own keep by producing goods of economic value. There are hints too that, not unexpectedly, they welcomed a certain amount of work with their hands as a relief from study sessions or from boredom and as a time for reflection. The cadres for their part could, by observing the prisoners engaged in labour, infer the quality and extent of their change in attitude and judge their willingness to contribute to the socialist future of China. Like good Marxists, the cadres knew that in the testing of truth subjective intentions were not sufficient and the only worthy criterion was practice. On their assessment, cadres based their recommendations regarding the prisoners' readiness for release.

To demonstrate that the new socialist China was something worth working for, and to provide an evidential basis for the beliefs about it that were being promoted, inspection tours were arranged for the prisoners. Some visits were to places in the neighbourhood of the prison, while others extended to far-distant cities where accommodation would be arranged in good hotels. The tours were designed to acquaint the prisoners with recent developments in industry, mining, agriculture, transport, housing and education, and generally to convince them that the revolutionary government was competent to achieve the goals it had set for itself. They were also brought into contact with ordinary and apparently contented people so that their regret for having in the past been associated with the forces of reaction might be deepened and intensified.

It is evident then that, for these prisoners, there was a very carefully thought out form of organization, servicing a varied but coherent programme, administered in a subtle, consistent, disciplined and seemingly humane fashion by officers imbued with a perceptive understanding of the working of the mind. As to whether these officers were engaged in an activity that we should be prepared to name as education or whether we should want to apply some depreciatory label is a question taken up in the next chapter.

12 RE-EDUCATION AND FREEDOM

Revolutions are not made with rose-water.

(Sebastien Chamfort)

This chapter examines further the nature of the process that was described in the last, the purpose motivating those who devised and implemented it and the state of mind and circumstances of the prisoners in the years following their release. In the course of this examination it will touch on the questions of indoctrination and human rights.

Former commandant Jin Yuan, it will be recalled, saw the Fushun prison as 'not just a place where criminals were rounded up, but a place of education, adhering to Chairman Mao's principle that every person is capable of being reformed' (p.62). The same principle underlay the remarks in 1960 of Xie Juezai, the then President of the Supreme People's Court. His address to the National People's Congress when he referred to the 1959 amnesty has already been quoted at the outset. Xie expressed pride in the achievement of having been able 'to reform war criminals into new people'. This was the amnesty releasing Du Yuming and Song Xilian as well as the former Emperor.

Whatever the final verdict must be about the possibility and the reality of turning prisoners into 'new socialist men', there is no doubt of the efforts in this direction. All those interviewed, whether former prisoners or prison officers, testified to the considerable time set aside in the daily prison programmes for self-examination, study and discussion and to the careful organization of this time, all directed at developing attitudes favourable to the Communist regime.

There is good evidence, too, of measures to ensure good health through medical care, proper diet and hygienic conditions and to make opportunities for physical, recreational and vocational activities. Further, there was a deliberate attempt to inform prisoners about current affairs and recent developments through newspapers, lectures and visits. Here were the elements of an all-round programme that witnessed to someone's belief that it was possible to effect deep changes in people. The programme addressed itself to all aspects of the personality of its 'pupils': their beliefs and attitudes, their knowledge and skills and their physical well-being. Whatever the final decision on the correct label to apply to this programme, one point is clear at this stage of the discussion. As they were described to us, the various measures added up to more than mere ornamentation or window-dressing. They were, I am convinced, of the essence.

A stated condition for the release of a prisoner was that he had 'truly reformed'. There is probably a complex of reasons why imprisonment periods varied in length. The propaganda value and status of the prisoner would form part of this complex, and so would changes in government or Party policy and other events external to the prison. It was the reform criterion, however, that figured prominently in the explanations we were offered whenever we asked about this. Certainly there appears to have been no correlation between the number or the nature of the alleged crimes and the term of imprisonment. Duan Kewen (1978, Article 16), who saw six batches of his fellow prioners released from Fushun between 1959 and 1966 made this observation, which accords with the official policy as stated by Supreme Court President, Xie Juezai:

> Our pardons are granted largely according to whether or not a criminal has really changed over. In other words, the important thing is whether or not a criminal has shown, both in politics and ideology and also in actual deeds, that he has truly reformed. What we have been doing is in the interest of the people throughout the country and completely conforms with the lofty ideal of our Party to reform mankind and transform society.
>
> (NCNA, 9 April 1960; trans. in *CB*, 624, 30 June 1960: 18)

We cannot claim that the experience of the former prisoners whom we interviewed was typical of that of political prisoners in other prisons and detention centres throughout China. We can however compare it with what was expected of the people at large.

Speaking in 1950 of the Method of Criticism and Self-Criticism, Mao declared,

> This is an excellent method, which impels everyone of us to uphold truth and rectify error, and it is the only correct method for all revolutionary people to educate and remould themselves in a people's state. The people's democratic dictatorship uses two methods. Towards the enemy, it uses the method of dictatorship, that is, for as long a period of time as is necessary it does not permit them to take part in political activity and compels them to obey the the law of the People's Government, to engage in labour, and,

through such labour, be transformed into new men. Towards the people, on the contrary, it uses the method of democracy and not of compulsion, that is, it must necessarily let them take part in political activity and does not compel them to do this or that but uses the method of democracy to educate and persuade. Such education is self-education for the people, and its basic method is criticism and self-criticism.

(*SW*, V:40)

Although the handful of prisoners whom we interviewed had been 'enemies of the people', the process to which they were expected to submit during the period their liberty was denied them was based on that same faith in the feasibility of reform as were the numerous mass mobilization campaigns mounted nationwide to raise the political consciousness and direct the actions and attitudes of the people themselves.

It cannot of course be maintained that there is no element of reprisal in a measure so extreme as imprisonment, especially when that imprisonment might last for the better part of an individual's adult life. Indeed the Statute on Punishment for Counter-revolutionary Activity, promulgated and made effective on 21 February 1951, speaks clearly of punishment by death, by life imprisonment and by terms of imprisonment graduated according to the seriousness of the crime. Added to these are deprivation of political rights and confiscation of personal property (*RMRB*, 22 February 1951; *SCMP*, 72, 23-4 February 1951). This statute, however, must be balanced by reference to the Statute on Labour Re-education (promulgated 7 September 1954), which speaks of 'the goal of transforming criminals into new persons' (Article 25), of persuading them 'to renounce the thought of crime and create a new conception of morality' (Article 26), and of lightening or cancelling a penalty if a prisoner 'indicates genuine repentance' (Article 73). It is largely the spirit of this act that ruled the prison experiences of the men we interviewed. To have served a principal purpose of reprisal, the atmosphere and routine must surely have been very different. Even when Duan Kewen wrote about the rough handling he received in the early years of his detention, he acknowledged that this arose in response not to his alleged offences under the Guomindang, but to his reluctance to co-operate in the reform programme itself.

Certainly the prisoners were expected to repudiate their former way of life and the crimes they were alleged to have committed against the people, but this was to be but a step in their own reformation.

The former prisoners examined in this study, having been put into prison, found themselves caught up in a strategy that demanded of them that they reassess their past and prepare themselves in health, knowledge and attitude for the future. On release, if they elected to remain in the new China, they would be assisted to play a positive role in its support and progress. If the policy informing this strategy was one of reprisal, carrying it into effect must have constituted one of the most sophisticated retaliations in history. But if the dominant purpose of imprisonment was to facilitate the eventual re-entry of former reactionaries into the new society, it still does not necessarily follow that the process was one to which the label of education should be attached.

Something will now be said about the nature of the educational process in which the prison tutors engaged their charges and of how far accusations against them of indoctrination or brain-washing may be justified. This discussion will bear in turn on the question of the prisoners' human rights.

I propose to start in a context familiar to educational philosophers of the West. In the liberal-democratic tradition, the teacher's ultimate intention is that the pupil will become a self-actuated independent individual, and he will hold to this intention even in the face of the possibility that his pupil may adopt beliefs and attitudes at variance with his own. This teacher teaches in such a way that all of his subject matter and all of his values remain open to question, to evidence and to alternative interpretations. He abandons any pretensions to either omniscience or omnipotence. The perfect classroom model in this respect reflects the democratic ideal of society at large. Confronted with views or attitudes that he finds unpalatable, the teacher is in the same position as any citizen in the liberal-democratic tradition who disagrees with another about what is best for society. Democracy, as we have come to understand the concept, denies the right to anyone to reshape an imperfect world if, in so doing, he must override the personal rights of someone else who prefers the world as it is. More important than to put the world right is to respect the integrity of others, even if this means that the world must stay imperfect. This is the paradox of democracy, and, to the extent that any teacher, in attempting to break the paradox, departs from the ideal and fails to safeguard the integrity of his pupils as human persons, he lays himself open to the charge of unacceptable behaviour or intention, a charge of indoctrination using the term in its pejorative sense. If the pupil is already a mature adult, some accusers might want to use the even more depreciatory term, brain-washing, implying that a more ruthless and intense attack may be needed to implant the desired belief than is the case with children. As I am here concerned primarily with intentions and only incidentally with methods, I shall regard the two terms as meaning essentially the same.

In considering the Chinese prison study programme from this point of view it is important to distinguish two questions. There is first the question of the extent to which our own beliefs and attitudes accord with those held by the Communist leadership and purveyed by the prison tutors. There is a tendency on the part of some who find themselves not in accord to make the accusation of indoctrination on that score. But this is merely to use the term as an expression of dislike or disapprobation arising out of a difference of opinion, which is altogether a very common state of affairs and surely not in itself reprehensible no matter how important the difference may be held to be. The more serious question from the point of view of the personal integrity of the prisoners relates to the intentions of the Communist leaders and their representatives. Did they intend that, as a result of the self-criticisms, study sessions, tours and the like, the prisoners should come to hold certain beliefs and attitudes irrevocably and without further question, come what may in the future? If that was so, then, still arguing within the liberal-democratic tradition, that would indeed be reprehensible. Whatever the said beliefs and attitudes, such an intention would amount to an attack on the inherent rights and personality of their pupils.

There can be little doubt that, judged according to this argument, the process we have been examining, was one of indoctrination. Prisoners were expected to 'confess' all their past actions, even those that they did not themselves regard as 'wrong' and for which, therefore, they could feel no guilt. According to the views of their interrogator-confessors, actions committed in the name of the former government and its agencies were wrong by that circumstance alone and that is how the prisoners must come to view them.

The authorities were prepared to go to great lengths to check the accuracy of even the smallest details so that nothing might be omitted from the confessions. Only through accuracy and completeness could they judge, they said, a prisoner's sincerity and proper desire for re-education. Some anecdotes have already been related to illustrate the prison officers' persistence and diligence in obtaining an accurate confession. Pujie told how his brother kept back information about hidden valuables and the consequences of this; Shen Zui's story of the Mauser pistols was probably typical of his general obstinacy to reveal his past; it was probably Duan Kewen's reluctance to spell out his connection with the Guomindang secret service that resulted in his prolonged imprisonment. When we visited Fushun, J.P. was amazed to discover the detail in which his father's career, both public and domestic, was documented. One of the officers with whom we spoke, Sun Shiqiang, had been detailed to journey to Jiangxi province to check assertions in Hu senior's confessions. An accurate, detailed and genuine life-statement was, it is clear, regarded as an essential step in the process. Only having purged themselves and emptied their minds of the past were the prisoners then judged ready to receive the new doctrine, presented as one for which there could be no legitimate alternative. The indoctrination may not always have been wholly successful. Huang Wei, as we have seen, managed most of the time to keep his mind focused elsewhere than on political study; Cai Xingsan adhered throughout to his pre-1949 views on the Soviet Union; Duan Kewen learnt neither sympathy for the Communist cause nor support for the present government. The intention, nevertheless, was undoubtedly there on the part of the tutors.

The conclusion that indoctrination was attempted is, it should be emphasized, based on this assessment of the intention held by the tutors and their higher authorities and not on the means they used or advocated in the process. With regard to the latter, apart from the fact of imprisonment itself, nearly all the evidence points to non-oppressive, non-coercive methods having been followed. The method in general was one of persuasion (*shuofu*: literally to convince through talk), not of coercion (*qiangzhi*). Apart from Duan's testimony of the treatment he received before he was admitted to Fushun, there was no hint of harshness or brutality, no use of solitary confinement, no punitive restriction of diet, no use of labour as punishment and no administration of drugs. Indeed, the Fushun staff seem to have been possessed of extraordinary patience coupled with an impressive insight into human motivation and behaviour and a nice subtlety of approach.

I wish now to relate the allegation of indoctrination more closely to the question of human rights and then to see whether a consideration of traditional Chinese thought might cast a different light on the whole matter than is evident from the liberal-democratic viewpoint.

If the reason for imprisoning former leaders was less to exact retribution than it was to remould their thinking, there would appear to be a prima facie case for accusing the Communist leadership of an infringement of human rights of the most serious kind. As Amnesty International has put it, 'The treatment of political offenders [in the People's Republic of China] results from a consistent policy of denying to individuals the right to deviate from standards of behaviour defined by official policy' (Amnesty International, 1978: xii). A reading of official documents from a Western viewpoint certainly leads to this conclusion. It is as if error, in the personification of 'enemies of the people', had no rights. Mao Zedong did not ignore the concept of human rights but he rejected rights as the natural attribute of all.

'The natural rights of man' represents, of course, an erroneous line of thought. Is there such a thing as rights bestowed by nature? Isn't it man who bestows rights on man? Were the rights we enjoy bestowed by nature? Our rights were bestowed by the common people, and primarily by the working class and the poor and lower-middle peasants.
(Mao Zedong in a speech at Hangzhou 21 December 1965, quoted in Schram, 1974: 234)

This view that rights might be accorded by and to particular classes in society is foreign enough to the accepted way of thought in the West, but what is even more to the point for the present discussion is that, in Chinese writing both traditional and modern, the very notion itself of rights was nearly always absent from discussions of the nature of society and the relations between its members. We in the West have become so accustomed to attributing fundamental human rights to individual citizens, at least notionally, and to believing that respect for human rights should be a matter of international observance and responsibility, that we may not stop to consider whether such a mode of thinking might not be culture bound.

For two thousand years and more, Chinese thinkers have analyzed the relationship between people without recourse to the concept of rights. The Confucian ethic was expounded in terms of wisdom (*zhi*), benevolence (*ren*), loyalty (*yi*), propriety (*li*), and sincerity (*xin*). The notion of rights did not appear, although it may be argued to be inherent in Confucius's unifying principle of reciprocity (*shu*): 'What you do not yourself desire, do not put before others' (*Analects*, XV: 23). This argument falls short, however, of what is needed to assert the existence of rights in the sense we wish to adopt; for, under the principle of reciprocity, any rights that one person might be thought to have would be dependent on the duties of others. In a hierarchical society, duties are far from equally distributed.

Mao Zedong himself was no stranger to the classics. Speaking only a couple of months before the formal establishment of the People's Republic in 1949, he gave forewarning of the treatment that so-called 'enemies of the people' could expect at the hands of the new regime.

> We definitely do not apply a policy of benevolence to the reactionaries and towards the reactionary activities of the reactionary classes. Our policy of benevolence is applied only within the ranks of the people, not beyond them to the reactionary activities of reactionary classes.
>
> (*SW*, IV: 418)

Even when he went on to refer to the 'people' as distinct from their enemies, it was not to speak of their rights as individuals, but to assure them that collectively as a class they could look forward to the protection of the State. Mao's use of the word for the Confucian virtue *ren* would not be lost on many in his audience. In the 'democratic dictatorship' about to be set up, an individual's protection was to lie not in some notion of rights universally accorded to all, but in the humaneness and good will of those holding power.

This is in line with a long tradition and, although it is not intended by this observation to condone the denial of human rights to any person, it does help us understand official Chinese policy and practice and may help explain why some traditionally-educated individuals, finding themselves on the wrong side of the political wall, have been able to accept without reproach the treatment meted out to them.

The concept of rights arrived much later to China than it did to the Western democracies. Professor Wang Gungwu, Director of the Research School of Pacific Studies at the Australian National University, made this point when he delivered the 1979 Morrison lecture (Wang, 1980). He reminded his audience that there was no word in the Chinese classical texts to service the notion of rights as it occurs in (say) the United Nations Declaration of Human Rights. The word *quanli*, coming into the language in the nineteenth century in the context of *national* rights and sovereignty, gradually became accepted in the twentieth century as a general term for the idea of rights as encountered in modern Western books of law, history and philosophy. But *quanli* in its literal meaning of power accompanied by profit was, Wang Gungwu cautioned, often used in contrast to the classical social virtue of *renyi*. For the classically educated, therefore, it would not be something actively to be sought after or promoted. Nor is there surrounding *quanli* any of the connotation of absolute or universal as there is when Western writers use the term 'rights' derived from phrases like 'natural rights'.

Thus, in trying to understand the reform of political prisoners in Chinese terms, it is well to remember with Professor Wang Gungwu that, whereas Chinese society 'clearly underlined the importance of duties for thousands of years, [it] did not seem to have developed a matching concern for rights' (ibid.: 5).

Nor can it easily be imagined that the new rulers in the 1950s would have found it a matter of any great urgency that 'benevolence', let alone rights, be extended to those formerly powerful elements in society who had so actively opposed the establishment of the socialist state. It is to be counted remarkable that, in a period when so much political energy had to be extended in reconstructing society, the new leaders should deem it important to develop a positive method of handling their foremost opponents and to gather them up too in the work of reconstruction.

The prison methods that were followed can now be put into a different light. The whole re-education process with its confessions, criticisms and study sessions was undertaken with the intention not of destroying people but in anticipation of their reinstatement into society. Many Chinese would find nothing reprehensible in the attempt to mould people to fit a particular conception of the state. It is in line with what Donald Munro (1977: 178) has called the Maoist Concept of Man. In some of its aspects this concept has a longer history in China than Mao Zedong Thought especially in its blurring of the distinction between public and private domains, a distinction so dear to the heart of the Western individualist. Confucian man could not imagine any more than socialist man that he had any personal choice in the values and duties associated with his place in society. Add to this prescription of roles the belief that a person's fundamental thoughts can be changed and that class-consciousness is something that can be learned, and a revolutionised and co-ordinated society could be grasped as a possibility for the near future. China needed no longer be Sun Yat-sen's sad 'tray of loose sand'. The violence of the early stages of the revolution would of course be traumatic, even fatal, for some. The eighteenth-century French moralist, Nicolas-Sebastien Chamfort, declared that 'revolutions are not made with rose-water'. Mao's twentieth-century definition is even more forceful when he contrasts the act of revolution with the Confucian virtues:

A revolution is not a dinner party, or writing an essay, or painting a picture, or doing embroidery; it cannot be so refined, so leisurely and gentle, so temperate, kind, courteous, restrained and magnanimous. A revolution is an insurrection, an act of violence by which one class overthrows another.

(Report on an Investigation of the Peasant Movement in Hunan', March 1927. *SW*, I:28)

But after the violence could come the reconstruction. Those who opposed the revolution would have to be reformed if the newly reconstructed society was to have a common set of values, awareness and aspirations. The degree of reformation judged to be necessary would vary with the circumstances surrounding individual cases, great importance being assumed by class background and by the individual's potential to influence others. Rank and file soldiers and NCOs from the Nationalist Army, coming for the most part from peasant and working class backgrounds, were deemed to need little in the way of re-education before they could take their place in the new society and be entrusted with its defence. In the early 1950s, the People's Liberation Army had some 7.5 million men of whom half had been Nationalist troops and, of the intervention force sent into Korea in 1950, the proportion of former Nationalist soldiers ranged as high as 50 to 70 per cent (George, 1967: 83). But the captured Guomindang generals were from a different class and their remoulding was, as we have seen, an exercise requiring much greater diligence.

In trying to assess the reform process that we have been examining, it is important to remember that everyone without exception in the new society was expected to take political education seriously. Speaking on the eve of the declaration of the People's Republic and explaining the role of the state in making thought reform possible, Mao said:

The people's state protects the people. Only when the people have such a state can they educate and remould themselves by democratic methods on a country-wide scale, with everyone taking part, and shake off the influence of domestic and foreign reactionaries . . ., rid themselves of the bad habits and ideas acquired in the old society, not allow themselves to be led astray by the reactionaries, and
continue to advance — to advance towards a socialist and communist society.

('On the People's Democratic Dictatorship', 30 June 1949. *SW*, IV: 418)

Mao went on to speak of the re-education of members of the reactionary classes: 'Propaganda and educational work will be done among them too' — but by imposition rather than persuasion. What is being emphasized here is that, apart from the degree and manner of compulsion used, many elements of the prison methods as already described were reflections of methods with widespread adoption in the nation at large.

This chapter has been premised on the belief that a judgement about the re-education methods followed in respect of the former prisoners we have been studying depends, at least in part, on an assessment of intentions and that this, in turn, is very dependent on the philosophical viewpoint of the person making the judgement. Liberal-democratic notions of individual rights, privacy and liberty of thought, accepted so widely in the West, did not have the same force in China as the leaders of its revolution faced the problem of social and national reconstruction following 150 years of despair, turbulence, corruption, subjugation and indecision. They chose a totalist solution. If we find that unpalatable, if we are repelled by deliberate attempts at indoctrination and thought control, we can perhaps speculate on what might have been the alternative. We can still have regard, too, for the fact that it has been possible to document the existence, within the limitations of that context, of people in authority who, motivated by sincerity to their cause, could act with thoughtfulness and human-heartedness towards those whom they took under their charge. But this thoughtfulness towards the individual sometimes took second place to the wish to make political capital.

The published comments of the authorities on the occasions of the several amnesties echo a pride in the reform methods to which the pardoned prisoners had been subjected. At the time of the second amnesty in November 1960, the official New China News Agency announced that

guided by revolutionary humanitarianism, patient education and reformation were carried out among war criminals during their imprisonment by the People's Government. The fact that these war criminals who had committed serious crimes have repented their crimes and turned over a new leaf proves once again the strength and correctness of the policy of the Chinese Communist Party and the People's Government of reforming criminals.

(*SCMP*, 2389, 2 December 1960: 1)

This pride is understandable. Men who were once in positions of military and civilian leadership on the side of the Guomindang were now prepared to support their former adversaries, even to thank them.

The pride, however, was not always solely in the reform process itself. It was often linked, in the official statements, with a more generalized pride in the superiority of Party and Government. Another part of the announcement just quoted referred back to the first amnesty in these terms:

> The publication and execution of the first order granting pardons showed the prosperity of the country, the unprecedented consolidation of the State power of the people's democratic dictatorship and the victory of the policy of the Chinese Communist Party and the People's Government of combining punishment and leniency and reform through labour with ideological education in dealing with criminals. (ibid.)

A similar statement by Hua Guofeng published at the time of the final amnesty in 1975 claimed that amnesty as a demonstration that 'our socialist Motherland is enjoying a greater stability and unity and that the dictatorship of the proletariat is more consolidated than ever before' (*CP*, 7, 1975: 42).

In these statements there was no hint of concern for the individual, no recognition of the mental turmoil he must have suffered in the course of his conversion, no reference to the doubts he may still have had. Some nods in the direction of the individual would have softened the conclusion that the overriding concern of the authorities was to squeeze out of the amnesties the last ounce of political capital to be exploited both at home and abroad.

The most disturbingly touching of the photographs published to record the ceremonies and celebrations surrounding the 1975 amnesty was the one depicting Huang Wei receiving his notification of release. Under the solemn gaze of his former prison colleagues, he stands, body submissively inclined, eyes downcast, both arms outstretched to take his piece of paper. A former military general, a strong-willed independent thinker was singled out for this special act of humiliation and presented thus to the world to demonstrate in stark clarity where lay the locus of power in the new order.

Even should one hold a favourable view of the manner in which prisoners were treated before their release and however impressed one may be with their later opportunities for citizenship, it is difficult to avoid the suspicion that, in the publicity surrounding the releases, one has witnessed the mask slip from the leadership's cynicism. This does not mean that the whole reform process was shot through with disregard for the person or that there was nothing of true educational merit to be learnt from it. High authority made the decision to imprison and high authority made the decision to release. That it might seek to make political capital should not wholly determine one's view of what happened between and beyond these two decisions and of the motives and actions of the many others involved.

Having looked at the process and the motives behind it, we should now consider the product and ask ourselves what role the former prisoners themselves were playing in our interviews. Of the various possible answers to this question there are two extremes. At one extreme, it is possible that they were free agents responding of their own accord to an invitation to tell their story and glad to be doing so. At the other extreme, they might have been no more than tools of the Party machine acting either under duress to present a particular front or, as safely brainwashed puppets, quite unable to do other than echo the thoughts of their masters. To ask about the role these men were playing is to raise the question of the extent to which they were intellectually and emotionally liberated at the time of their physical release from prison. What is the nature of their commitment to the ruling ideology, policy and practice? What can be said about their independence of mind? Are they in any position to make a unique contribution to the future of China, or is their function now merely to assent to what others decree? In the figure of speech used by Lifton, has the kiln suffocated them?

> [The Chinese reformers] look upon human beings, at least implicitly, as wrongly moulded clay, needing only new moulds and proper remoulding from ideological potters – a remoulding process which they themselves are willing to pursue with the hottest of fires and the most suffocating of kilns.
>
> (Lifton, 1967: 525)

It is scarcely possible, on the basis of the interviews and the informal conversations at dinner, to pinpoint with accuracy the position between the extremes where the truth must lie, but my estimation would place it nearer the positive end of the scale. Du Yuming, Song Xilian, Shen Zui and Pujie were especially good-humoured and at ease while telling their stories. They had had of course plenty of time to adjust to

their new life. Nearly two decades had elapsed between release and interview. General Du had, it seems, been resigned to his position from the
outset. Defeated so often on the battlefield, he was happy enough
after capture to be carried along by history. Could he be called a tool
of the Communist Party? Possibly, but he seemed neither 'brainwashed'
nor to be under duress. Neither he himself nor his colleagues when
speaking about him gave any hint that he had ever resisted reform
efforts or made any sort of fuss. He is now a member of the National
People's Congress. Major-General Shen Zui in his recital enjoyed
painting an evil picture of his pre-conversion self. (One was reminded
of the saying that there is no more unbearable saint than a reformed
sinner.) He surely had retained his personality for which his present
position permitted a more overt expression than had his circumscribed
existence as an under-cover agent. Present fame coming as the sweet
fruit of past notoriety gave no cause for bitterness. Pujie, former
prince, was clearly at ease, well dressed, intelligent and well preserved
physically. He had escaped the glare and the propaganda pressure
experienced by his brother, the Emperor. He is now a deputy to the
National People's Congress.

Of the more recently released men, Cai Xingsan was the youngest.
At 59 he was still youthful when we saw him in Hong Kong. Although
he had elected to live outside of the People's Republic, he appeared
to harbour no resentment against those who had been in charge of him
in prison. He seemed also to be on favourable terms with the Chinese
authorities, having through his Hong Kong-based company negotiated
business contracts with them. He has visited Peking at least once since
we talked with him. His behaviour was that of a fully rational and
confident person. At the other end of the age scale was General Huang
Wei. Strong-willed, he had resisted any assault on his intellect. He was
still good-humoured enough to share a joke, but he was more apt than
the others to be agitated by his memories. In the play for his
commitment it had been his emotions, not his intellect, that had been
trumped. Zhang Jingzhu, away from the direct eye of officialdom
during interview, was more ready than the others to allow a certain
weariness to creep into his tale. It is surprising there was not more
weariness considering the ages of these men. Apart from Cai, their
ages in January 1979 ranged from 65 to 75 and, with that in mind and
that they now lead regular, protected lives, one can see little cause why
they should speak unfavourably of their present situation. But that is
not to see them as being in a state of puppet-like dependence. In fact
they presented as men of such distinctive personalities that it is difficult

to imagine their ever having succumbed to an assault on their identity after the fashion described by Lifton. Of two Westerners, a priest and a doctor, who had undergone thought reform in China in the 1950s, Lifton asserted,

> each was reduced to something not fully human and yet not quite animal, no longer the adult and yet not quite the child; instead, an adult human was placed in the position of an infant or a sub-human animal, helplessly being manipulated by larger and stronger 'adults' or 'trainers'. Placed in this regressive stance, each felt himself deprived of the power, mastery, and selfhood of adult existence.
>
> (Lifton, 1967: 86)

Lifton here was describing the undermining of identity which he saw as an essential preliminary to the birth of the new man through thought reform. There remains the possibility that our men had been through this stage and had successfully negotiated the rebirth process. What if we had seen them during their imprisonment? Would they then, overwhelmed by guilt and shame and forced to the point of self-betrayal, have appeared as in Lifton's description or have been reduced to that sorry and pathetic specimen of humanity that French journalist, Lucien Bodard, interviewed in the Fushun prison in 1956? After meeting the former Emperor there he wrote of him as 'a thin sad-eyed man . . . who talked of nothing but his guilt . . . He sounded like a long-playing gramophone record' (Bodard, 1957: 140). None of the people we interviewed bore any resemblance to that picture of Puyi. If they had been through a transitional stage like that, as Lifton suggests, their reconstruction back into authentic personalities was indeed a remarkable feat of human engineering. My view is that, while the people we interviewed had doubtless shifted their views and attitudes to varying degrees, they had throughout retained their essential personalities.

. We now come to the point where we should reflect on the present place in society of these former top-ranking Nationalists. As has been reported in the biographical accounts, with the exception of Cai in Hong Kong, all the men we interviewed are currently members of the Chinese People's Political Consultative Conference (*Zhongguo Renmin Zhengzhi Xieshang Huiyi*). This membership might be regarded as both a continuation and a fulfilment of the prison re-education programme. It is clear that leaving prison with its orderly, purposeful and protective regimen was not for these men, as it often is for common criminals, like stepping into space. Theirs was a rehabilitation very close in meaning to that recorded in the Oxford English Dictionary: 'restoration by formal act or declaration (of a person degraded or attainted) to former privileges, rank, and possessions.' More significant than reunion with family and restoration of home life was this acceptance into the CPPCC. A united front organization, paralleling the People's Congresses at all levels — National, provincial and local — the *Zhengzhi*, as it is commonly abbreviated, has become the political and communal focus of their daily life. Within its protective bounds, they have found a refuge in regular discussion meetings and in the pursuit and development of activities that can be seen not only as of value to the nation but probably also as an extension of the cathartic experience of earlier confession writing. I refer to archival work and the writing of the history of campaigns and movements in which these men played such prominent parts. The CPPCC has helped preserve (if not reshape) the identity of these men, providing them with tangible means of working out a commitment to the new society within a mutually reinforcing group. Looked at from the point of view of the authorities, this has been an essential development from the intensive re-education carried on inside the prison. That it also possesses something of the nature of a true rehabilitation to former status is suggested by the observation that the level at which a former prisoner has been absorbed into the CPPCC is related to what that former status was. This question of status is deserving of further attention than given in this study. It is intriguing and to some extent disturbing to find that, throughout all the thought reform and re-education supposedly directed at producing a new class-consciousness, there remained with each one of the high-ranking officers and functionaries the distinct flavour of the status associated with their pre-Liberation positions.

One is led to the conclusion in the long run that there is between leaders, even if representative of opposing political factions, a respect and an understanding that run deeper and persist longer than any ties between leader and led on either side. In spite of imprisonment, the men of this study are no strangers to privilege under the Communist regime, and one wonders how often they and their counterparts on the winning side give a thought to the millions of common soldiers who fought the battles for them. Just as a revolution is not a dinner party, so neither is a dinner party an occasion for taking a revolution seriously. Or so it would seem from an anecdote told by Felix Greene (1964: 34). In 1960, Greene was invited to the new Great Hall of the People to share in a banquet being given by Premier Zhou Enlai (Chou En-lai) in honour of guest-of-state, Field-Marshal Viscount Montgomery.

Among the guests were Du Yuming (Tu Yu-ming) recently released from prison and Chen Yi, war hero of the Communists. Greene tells of their meeting with the former allied Commander.

> The Prime Minister now turned to the generals who had risen from their chairs and were waiting to be introduced. Pointing to Tu Yu-ming and Chen Yi, the Prime Minister said, 'These two fought each other. This one lost.'
> 'How many men did you have?' Mongomery asked Tu.
> 'A million.'
> 'Why did you lose if you had a million men?'
> 'They all ran over to his side', said Tu, nodding towards Chen Yi.
> Chou En-lai threw back his head and laughed.

There is something very disturbing about that laugh.

EARLY REGULATIONS AND A CICRC BULLETIN

In November-December 1952, workers' organizations in Hong Kong and Taiwan brought a complaint before the Paris-based Commission Internationale Contre le Régime Concentrationnaire (CICRC) against forced labour and concentration camps in the People's Republic of China. After some preliminary investigations, the CICRC sent a letter to Premier Zhou Enlai informing him of the complaints laid and seeking his permission for a delegation to inspect all correction camps, prisons and penal institutions or institutions of forced labour that might exist in the People's Republic. This letter was submitted at Geneva on 11 June 1954.

Not receiving a reply from the Chinese authorities, CICRC published a bulletin in December 1954 (CICRC, 1954). This was followed four years later by a White Paper on the subject (CICRC, 1958). In the bulletin two Chinese documents relating to 'forced labour' were discussed. They were 'Regulations relating to units in charge of the re-education through labour in the PRC' (adopted by the Administrative Council of the Government on 26 August 1954), and 'Provisional measures concerning the release of criminals undergoing re-education through labour at the expiration of their sentence and their placement in employment.' Both of these documents had been made public by the New China News Agency in Peking on 7 September 1954. The same day, the News Agency had published a commentary from the Minister of Public Security, Luo Ruiqing, entitled 'Explanation of the draft regulations concerning units of re-education through labour.' The *People's Daily* (*Renmin Ribao*) of 9 September had devoted its editorial to 'Realizing completely the politics of the units re-educating criminals through labour.' These various articles had their foundation in the Common Programme of the Chinese People's Political Consultative Conference promulgated in September 1949. It was this Programme that acted as provisional constitution for the People's Republic until 1954. Article 7 of the Common Programme provided for reform through labour with the intention of making new men out of reactionaries, feudal landlords and the bureaucratic-capitalistic high functionaries of the Guomindang. The CICRC bulletin pointed out that the two regulations referred to above systematized the 'extremely rich experience' of five years.

100

As early as 23 July 1950, the Administrative Council had published, over the signature of Zhou Enlai, the first 'Regulation concerning the suppression of counter-revolutionaries'; but the most important text for the period up to September 1954 was promulgated on 21 February 1951 under the title 'Regulation of the People's Republic of China governing the punishment of counter-revolutionaries' (*RMRB*, 22 February 1951; *SCMP*, 72, 23-4 February 1951). This set of 21 articles was to have wide applicability. The crime of counter-revolution – that of conspiring against or sabotaging the people's democratic dictatorship – was to be denounced wherever it might occur: in political action in general, in administration, in business, in the army. Further, the articles were to be retroactive: Article 7.3 castigated those who filled responsible positions in counter-revolutionary organizations before the Communists' arrival to power, and Article 18 stated explicitly that 'the provisions of this Regulation are applicable to the counter-revolutionary criminals who committed an offence before the promulgation of the said Regulation.'

Herein lay the statutory basis for the treatment administered to the high-ranking counter-revolutionaries who are the subject of this book.

EXAMPLE OF OFFICIAL ANNOUNCEMENTS RELATING TO AN AMNESTY

The following statments relating to the 1960 amnesty were released (in English) by the New China News Agency in Peking.

November 19, 1960

The Standing Committee of the National People's Congress at its 32nd session this afternoon adopted a decision to grant pardons to those war criminals of the Chiang Kai-shek clique and the puppet 'Manchukuo' who have really changed and behaved well after a certain period of reformation. The decision was made after a discussion of the State Council's proposal to grant pardons to such war criminals.

(*SCMP*, 2384, 24 November 1960: 1)

November 19, 1960

Decree on special pardons by the Chairman of the People's Republic of China: In accordance with a decision taken at the 32nd session of the standing committee of the 2nd National People's Congress, special pardon is hereby granted to war criminals of the Chiang Kai-shek clique and the puppet 'Manchukuo' who have really forsaken the evil to follow the good.

One. War criminals of the Chiang Kai-shek clique and the puppet 'Manchukuo' who have served fully ten years in person and really forsaken the evil to follow the good shall be freed.

Two. [Some to have their death sentence commuted to life imprisonment.]

Three. [Some to have their sentence of life imprisonment commuted to a limited term.]

This order shall be carried out by the Supreme People's Court and Higher People's Court.

(*SCMP*, 2384, 24 November 1960: 2)

November 28, 1960

The Supreme People's Court today pardoned and released the second group of war criminals who have really repented and turned over a new leaf, in accordance with the order of the Chairman of the PRC on granting pardon, issued on 19 November.

Altogether fifty war criminals were granted pardons and released in this group. Forty-five of them were war criminals of the Chiang Kai-shek clique, four of the puppet 'Manchukuo' and one of the puppet 'Inner Mongolian Autonomous Government'.

The Chairman of the PRC issued the first order granting pardons to war criminals on September 19, 1959. The order was executed by the Supreme People's Court and the first group of 33 war criminals were granted pardons last December. The publication and execution of the first order granting pardons showed the prosperity of the country, the unprecedented consolidation of the State power of the people's democratic dictatorship and the victory of the policy of the Chinese Communist Party and the People's Government of combining punishment with leniency and reforms through labour with ideological education in dealing with criminals.

In the past year, among the war criminals still in prisons, there are some who have also shown that they are repenting and turning over a new leaf. In accordance with the recent second order of pardons of the Chairman of the PRC, organs of the People's Government in charge of war criminals have carried out an overall examination of the records of the imprisoned war criminals, and decided, with the approval of the Supreme People's Court, to grant pardons and release an additional fifty war criminals . . . .

[List, including:]
Shen Tsui [Shen Zui], Major-General, Director of the Yunnan Branch of the KMT secret service organization, the Bureau of Confidential Information.
Aisin Ghiorroh Puchieh [Pujie], Aide-de-camp of the 'Royal Court' of the puppet 'Manchukuo' . . .

These 50 war criminals granted pardons and released had all committed serious crimes against the people in the past. They were taken prisoner by the PLA during the war of liberation and were imprisoned over ten years. Guided by revolutionary humanitarianism, patient education and reformation were carried out among the war criminals during their imprisonment by the People's Government. The fact that these war criminals who had committed serious crimes have repented their crimes and turned over a new leaf proves once again the strength and correctness of the policy of the Chinese Communist Party and the People's Government of reforming criminals. On 28 November, the Supreme People's Court and higher people's courts in various places convened general meetings in the organs in charge of war criminals on the granting of pardons and release at which all imprisoned war criminals were present. The lists of war criminals granted pardon and release were made public and the notification of the granting of pardons were issued to them.

(SCMP, 2389, 2 December 1960: 1)

BIBLIOGRAPHY

1. Publications Cited in the Text

CB   *Current Background*, Hong Kong: US Consulate General.
CP   *China Pictorial*, Peking.
CR   *China Reconstructs*, Peking.
GMRB *Guangming Ribao.*
NCNA New China News Agency.
RMRB *Renmin Ribao (People's Daily)*, Peking.
SCMP *Survey of China Mainland Press*, Hong Kong: US Consulate General.
SW   *Selected Works.* See Mao, below.

Aisin-Gioro Pu Yi. *From Emperor to Citizen*, English trans. by W.J.F. Jenner, 2 vols. (Peking: Foreign Languages Press, 1964-5)
Amnesty International. *Political Imprisonment in the People's Republic of China* (London: Amnesty International Publications, 1978)
Analects. See Legge
Bao Ruowang (Jean Pasqualini) & Chelminski, Rudolph. *Prisoner of Mao* (New York: Coward, McCann & Geohegan, 1973)
Belden, Jack. *China Shakes the World* (Harmondsworth: Pelican, 1973)
Bodard, Lucien. *La Chine de la Douceur* (Paris: Gallimard, 1957)
Cai Xingsan. 'Fang modai huangdi Puyide baodi – Pujie' (A visit to the former emperor Puyi's brother, Pujie), *Jing Bao (The Mirror)* (Hong Kong, May 1979), 12-14
——. 'Fang modai huangdi Puyide baodi – Pujie' (A visit to the former emperor Puyi's brother, Pujie), continued *Jing Bao (The Mirror)* (Hong Kong, June 1979), 24-25
——. 'Yuan Guomindang jiangjun Huang Wei xiang gao keyan' (Former KMT general Huang Wei likes doing scientific research), *Jing Bao (The Mirror)* (Hong Kong, August 1979), 52-5
——. 'Yi "Fushun zhanfan guanlisuo"' (A recollection of the Fushun war criminals administration centre), *Jing Bao (The Mirror)* (Hong Kong, September 1979), 58-9
——. 'Zhonggong duiyu "zhanfan" de chuli' (The Chinese Communists' treatment of 'war criminals'), *Jing Bao (The Mirror)* (Hong Kong, October 1979), 50-3
China Directory 1979 (Tokyo: Radio Press Inc., September 1978)

CICRC (Commission Internationale Contre Le Régime Concentrationnaire). *Bulletin d'Information* (Paris: Centre International d'Edition et de Documentation, 1954)

———. *Livre Blanc sur le Travail Forcé dans la R.P.C.* (Paris: Centre International d'Edition et de Documentation, 1958)

Duan Kewen. *Zhanfan Baishu (The Narration of a War Criminal)* (Taipei: Lianjing Publishing Co., March 1978 (first part) and January 1980 (second part))

George, Alexander L. *The Chinese Communist Army in Action: The Korean War and its Aftermath* (New York & London: Columbia University Press, 1967)

Greene, Felix. *The Wall Has Two Sides: A Portrait of China Today* (London: Jonathan Cape, 1964)

Guillermaz, Jacques. *The Chinese Communist Party in Power, 1949-1976*, trans. by Anne Destenay (Folkestone, England: Dawson, 1976)

Kwei, Chung-gi. *The Kuomintang-Communist Struggle in China, 1922-1949* (The Hague: Martinus Nijhoff, 1970)

Legge, James. *The Chinese Classics. Vol. I: Confucian Analects, the Great Learning, and the Doctrine of the Mean* (Oxford: The Clarendon Press, 1893)

Lifton, Robert Jay. *Thought Reform and the Psychology of Totalism. A Study of 'Brainwashing' in China* (Harmondsworth: Penguin, 1967)

Liu, F.F. *A Military History of Modern China 1924-1949* (Princeton, NJ: Princeton University Press, 1956)

Lo Kuang-pin & Yang Yi-yen. *Red Crag* (English version of *Hong Yan*) (Peking: Foreign Languages Press, 1978)

McAleavy, Henry. *A Dream of Tartary: The Origins and Misfortunes of Henry P'u Yi* (London: George Allen & Unwin, 1963)

Mao Zedong (Mao Tse-tung). *Selected Works* (Peking: Foreign Languages Press, Vol. I 1965, Vol. II 1965, Vol. III 1965, Vol. IV 1961, Vol. V 1977)

Munro, Donald J. *The Concept of Man in Contemporary China* (Ann Arbor: The University of Michigan Press, 1977)

Sargant, William. *Battle for the Mind. A Physiology of Conversion and Brain-washing* (London: Heinemann, 1957)

Schram, Stuart. *Mao Tse-tung Unrehearsed. Talks and Letters: 1956-71* (Harmondsworth: Penguin, 1974)

Shehui Fazhan Shi (The History of the Development of Society). Several revisions. Most recently issued in the Young People's Self Study Collection (Shanghai: The People's Publishing House, 1974)

Wang Gungwu. 'Power, Rights and Duties in Chinese History', *Australian Journal of Chinese Affairs, 3* (January 1980), 1-26
White, T.H. (ed.). *The Stilwell Papers* (New York: Sloane, 1948)

2. Other Relevant Publications

Blaustein, Albert. *Fundamental Legal Documents of Communist China* (Littleton, Colorado: Rothman & Co., 1962)
Bonnichon, André. *Law in Communist China* (The Hague: International Commission of Jurists, 1956)
Boorman, Howard & Howard, Richard C. (eds.). *Biographical Dictionary of Republican China*, 4 vols. (New York: Columbia University Press, 1967-71)
Chassin, Lionel Max. *The Communist Conquest of China. A History of the Civil War, 1945-49*, trans. from the French by Timothy Osato & Louis Gelas (London: Weidenfeld and Nicolson, 1966)
Chen, Theodore H.E. *Thought Reform of the Chinese Intellectuals* (Hong Kong: Hong Kong University Press, 1960)
Cheng Shu-ping. *The Chinese Communist System of Reform Through Labour* (Republic of China: Asian People's Anti-Communist League, April 1978)
Cohen, Jerome A. *The Criminal Process in the People's Republic of China, 1949-63* (Cambridge, Mass.: Harvard University Press, 1968)
Festinger, Leon. *A Theory of Cognitive Dissonance* (Stanford: Stanford University Press, 1957)
Finkelstein, David. 'The Language of China's Criminal Law', *Journal of Asian Studies, 27*(3) (May 1968), 503-21
Grey, Anthony. *Hostage in Peking* (London: Michael Joseph, 1970)
Griffin, Patricia E. *The Chinese Communist Treatment of Counter-revolutionaries: 1924-1949* (Princeton, NJ: Princeton University Press, 1976)
Guillermaz, Jacques. *A History of the Chinese Communist Party 1921-1949* trans. by Anne Destenay (London: Methuen, 1972)
Houn, Franklin W. *To Change a Nation: Propaganda and Indoctrination in Communist China* (Michigan: Bureau of Social and Political Research, Michigan University, 1961)
Klein, D.W. & Clark, A.B. *Biographic Dictionary of Chinese Communism, 1921-1965*, 2 vols. (Cambridge, Massachusetts: Harvard University Press, 1971)
Lai Ying. *The Thirty-Sixth Way. A Personal Account of Imprisonment*

and Escape from Red China, trans., adapted and edited by Edward Behr & Sydney Liu (London: Constable, 1970)

Meerloo, J.A.M. *The Rape of the Mind* (New York: World Publishing Co., 1956), also as *Mental Seduction and Menticide. The Psychology of Thought Control and Brainwashing* (London: Jonathan Cape, 1957)

Mills, Harriet C. 'Thought Reform: Ideological Remolding in China', *Atlantic Monthly, 2041* (6) (December 1959), 71-7

Rickett, Allyn & Adele. *Prisoners of Liberation* (New York: Ankor Press/Doubleday, 1957, 1973)

Rokeach, Milton. *The Nature of Human Values* (New York: Free Press, 1973)

Schein, Edgar H. with Schneier, Inge & Barker, Curtis H. *Coercive Persuasion: A Socio-psychological Analysis of the 'Brainwashing' of American Civilian Prisoners by the Chinese Communists* (New York: Norton, 1971)

Sih, Paul K.T. (ed.). *Nationalist China during the Sino-Japanese War, 1937-1945* (New York: Exposition Press, 1977)

Tung, William L. *Revolutionary China. A Personal Account, 1926-1949* (New York: St Martin's Press, 1973)

USA. *Guide to Selected Legal Sources of Mainland China. A Listing of Laws and Regulations and Periodical Literature with a Brief Survey of the Administration of Justice by Tao-tai Hsia* (Washington: Library of Congress, 1967)

Wilson, Amy Auerbacher, Greenblatt, Sidney Leonard & Wilson, Richard Whittingham (eds.). *Deviance and Social Control in Chinese Society* (New York: Praeger, 1977)

Wilson, Richard W., Wilson, Amy A. & Greenblatt, Sidney L. (eds.). *Value Change in Chinese Society* (New York: Praeger, 1979)

CHINESE CHARACTER GLOSSARY

People

Aixinjueluo Pujie 爱新觉罗溥杰

Cai Ruoshu 蔡若曙

Cai Xingsan 蔡省三

Cai Zhicheng 蔡志程

Chen Yi 陈毅

Chun 醇（亲王）

Cixi 慈禧

Dai Li 戴笠

Deng Xiaoping 邓小平

Du Yuming 杜聿明

Duan Kewen 段克文

Guang Xu 光绪

Hu Lian 胡琏

He Long 贺龙

Hu Yunhong 胡逸鸿

Hua Guofeng 华国锋

Huang Botao 黄伯韬

Huang Minnan 黄敏南

Huang Wei 黄维

Huang Huinan 黄慧南

Huisheng 慧生

Husheng 嫮生

Jiang Jingguo 蒋经国

Jin Yuan 金元

Li Gongpu 李公仆

Liu Bocheng 刘伯诚

Liu Jiachang 刘家常

Liu Qinshi 刘勤实

Liu Ruming 刘汝明

Liu Xiang 刘湘

Lu Han 卢汉

Mao Zedong 毛泽东

Nie Rongzhen 聂荣臻

Nie Zhen 聂真

Pujie 溥杰

Puyi 溥仪

Shen Zui 沈醉

Song Xilian 宋希濂

Sun Chuanfang 孙传芳

Sun Shiqiang 孙世强

Wang Daojian 王道俭

Wen Yiduo 闻一多

Xie Juezai 谢觉哉

Xie Li 谢梨

Xuan Tong 宣统

Yang Hucheng 杨虎城

Yang Yong 杨勇

Yang Zhenning 杨振宁

Ye Jianying 叶剑英

Zai Tao 载涛

Li Yannian	李延年	Zhang Chunqiao	张春桥
Lin Biao	林彪	Zhang Guotao	张国焘
Zhang Jingzhu	张劲竹	Zhong Qinhua	钟钦华
Zhang Weizhou	张维周	Zhou Enlai	周恩来
Zhang Xueliang	张学良	Zhou Yanghao	周养浩
Zhang Xuesi	张学思	Zhu De	朱德
Zhang Zuolin	张作霖		

Places

Provinces

Anhui	安徽	Liaoning	辽宁
Guizhou	贵州	Shandong	山东
Hebei	河北	Sichuan	四川
Hubei	湖北	Taiwan	台湾
Hunan	湖南	Xinjiang	新疆
Jiangxi	江西	Yunnan	云南
Jilin	吉林	Zhejiang	浙江

Towns, Localities, etc.

Anshan	鞍山	Longhai	陇海
Bei Fu	北府	Leshan	乐山
Beiping	北平	Nanchang	南昌
Bengbu	蚌埠	Nanjing	南京
Changchun	长春	Pingdingshan	平顶山
Changsha	长沙	Ruijin	瑞金
Chengdu	成都	Shanghai	上海
Chongqing	重庆	Shangrao	上饶

Dadu	大渡	Shenyang	沈阳
Fushun	抚顺	Shuangduiji	双堆集
Ganzhou	赣州	Suxian	宿县
Guilin	桂林	Tiananmen	天安门
Hankou	汉口	Tianjin	天津
Harbin	哈尔滨	Wuhan	武汉
Huai	淮（海）	Xi'an	西安
Huguosi	护国寺	Xifeng	息烽
Jinan	济南	Xuzhou	徐州
Kunming	昆明	Yan'an	延安
Liaoxi	辽西		

Organizations, Institutions, Publications, etc.

Fudan 复旦

Fuguo Gong 护国公

Guomindang 国民党

Hong Yan 红岩

Jing Bao 镜报

Lujun daxuexiao jiaoyu kanling 陆军大学校教育纲领

Nei Wu Fu 内务府

Qing 清（朝）

Qinghua 清华

Shijie Ribao 世界日报

Zhanfan guanlisuo 战犯管理所

Zhongguo Renmin Zhengzhi Xieshang Huiyi

中国人民政治协商会议

Terms and Phrases

dui   队

fouding   否定

guanzhi   管制

hanyu pinyin   汉语拼音

jiantao   检讨

jiaoxin fang   交心房

jiaozui   交罪

laodong fuwu   劳动服务

laodong gaizao   劳动改造

laodong jiaoyang   劳动教养

laodong jineng   劳动技能

li   礼

liangtiao luxian   两条路线

piping he ziwo piping   批评和自我批评

quanli   权利

ren   仁

renyi   仁义

renzui   认罪

san guang zhengce   三光政策

san min zhuyi   三民主义

sheng huo hui   生活会

shu   想

shuoli douzheng hui   说理斗争会

taijiquan   太极拳

xiao dui hui   小队会

xin   信

yi   义

zhengzhi sixiang gaizao   政治思想改造

zhi   知

zhidaoyuan   指导员

zhuren   主任

zu   组

INDEX

With few exceptions, names of Chinese persons and places in the text have been romanised using *pinyin* transcription. Cross-references are included in the index for readers more familiar with Wade-Giles.

For Product Safety Concerns and Information please contact our EU
representative GPSR@taylorandfrancis.com
Taylor & Francis Verlag GmbH, Kaufingerstraße 24, 80331 München, Germany

www.ingramcontent.com/pod-product-compliance
Lightning Source LLC
Chambersburg PA
CBHW070858270326
41926CB00039B/3230